4.50

HENRY ALLINE

J. M. BUMSTED

Henry Alline
1748-1784

CANADIAN BIOGRAPHICAL STUDIES

UNIVERSITY OF TORONTO PRESS

CANADIAN
BIOGRAPHICAL
STUDIES

©   University of Toronto Press 1971
Printed in Canada
ISBN 0-8020-3247-8

FOR MY FATHER

FOREWORD

The *Canadian Biographical Studies* is allied with the project of the *Dictionary of Canadian Biography/ Dictionnaire biographique du Canada.*

These small volumes are designed primarily to interest the general reader, and they will be published in two languages. They seek to fill a gap in our knowledge of men who seemed often to be merely secondary figures, frequently non-political contributors to our regional and national experience in Canada. Our social, educational, and economic history may perhaps be better understood in their light.

In these *Studies,* the emphasis is upon an interpretation rather than a life. The limitation in size challenges the author to consider the best use of anecdote, description of place, reference to general history, and use of quotation. The general reader will be offered the fruits of recent research. Not all of the volumes will aim at full comprehensiveness and completeness: some may be followed later by larger and fuller studies of the subject. Many of the present studies, it is hoped, may suggest new interpretative possibilities not only about the central figure but about his period.

The editors have not followed two of Plutarch's chief standards: the subjects of these *Studies* have not been chosen only for their public virtue, or for their acknowledged distinction. Most of them lived out their lives in Canada, but for some their careers were conducted partly in other theatres. Some have been chosen because, though they were once widely known, they have since been undeservedly neglected. Some have been selected not for their obvious leadership or eminence, but because they were sufficiently prominent to represent some of the qualities that guided their age, men of significance if not of first prominence. Some have been grouped in studies that should throw light on interesting families, professional groups, or lobbies in our past.

Thus, the *Studies* present not biography alone, but social, economic and political history approached through the careers and ideas – acknowledged, but often unrecognized – of Canadians of many ranks and diverse times.

ALAN WILSON

CONTENTS

1

*The Scenes
and Pleasures of a
Country Life*

Henry Alline was born in Newport, Rhode Island, on 14 January 1748, and he died in North-Hampton, New Hampshire, on 28 January 1784. His lifespan thus fell far short of the biblical 'three score and ten,' but this was hardly deserving of comment in the 18th-century America of which Alline was a part. Life was hard, to call a doctor was more likely to kill than cure, and the risk of violent death was ever present. A bare recital of Alline's vital statistics fails totally to reveal how much accomplishment he had packed into a short life, or to indicate that the principal stage for his activities was not what is now the United States, but what is today Maritime Canada. Henry Alline is virtually unknown to Canadians of the present century, but the years in which he lived were particularly critical ones for Canada, and his career both mirrors and dominates a period of pioneer hardship, political crisis, and deep spiritual concern born of the uncertainties of human existence.

Alline's lifespan coincides almost exactly with the first wave of British settlement in Nova Scotia and the years of the American Revolution which represent such a watershed in Maritime development. Before the outbreak of the colonial rebellion, Nova Scotia had been settled principally by natives of New England as part of a general expansion of population in British North America which reached its peak just after the middle of the 18th century. That Alline was born in Rhode Island was of no great importance: Rhode Island and Nova Scotia were both parts of a great British empire, and their citizens all British subjects. After 1783, immigration to Maritime Canada would come from Loyalists displaced from the rebellious American colonies and from the British Isles, especially Scotland and Ireland. The unity of the empire would be broken, and Alline would die, although purely by accident, not on British soil, but on American. English Canadians have a general tendency to think of their history as beginning with the United Empire Loyalists, but the earlier New

England migration to the Maritimes was responsible for establishing Nova Scotia as a British colony and set in motion a good many of the fundamental ways of life which characterized Maritime Canada for generations to come. In this early history, the name of Henry Alline stands out, both because of his own participation in the process and problems of settlement and because of his assumption of leadership of the New England population during the trying times of the American Revolution.

Like most British subjects who settled in Nova Scotia before 1775, Henry Alline was a member of a venerable if not venerated New England family. His father, William Alline, had been born in Boston in 1714 and could trace his ancestry back to Isaac Allerton, one of the *Mayflower* passengers who had landed at Plymouth in 1620. William's second marriage – to Rebeccah Clark of Boston in 1738 – produced eight children, of whom Henry was the second-born.[1] William Alline's successive residences at Boston and Newport – New England's largest urban centres – suggest that he was not by profession a farmer. It is possible that William was associated with milling before his arrival in the Maritimes, since he later owned and operated a grain mill in Nova Scotia.

In his autobiography, the main source of information about his personal life, Henry Alline said little of his childhood in Newport. But he did contrast the lively urban activities of the Rhode Island city with the less exciting 'scenes and pleasures of a country life' in Nova Scotia.[2] Newport, after all, was one of British North America's most thriving urban communities. Built on the southern tip of 'Rhode Island,' a small island just off the mainland coast of the colony, Newport was an important seaport and manufacturing centre with a population of six thousand. The Alline family lived in the midst of the activity. Besides the bustle of the wharves and artisan shops, Newport had a variety of attractions. Unlike other New England colonies,

Rhode Island enjoyed almost complete religious toleration. As a result, the city had not only Puritan meeting-houses, but active communities of Baptists and Quakers, and even a synagogue of Sephardic Jews. One of North America's most inventive and original architects, Peter Harrison, was actively designing and constructing new buildings in Newport during Henry Alline's childhood days. The city had an outspoken newspaper in the *Newport Mercury*, was talking about founding a university, and enjoyed one of the finest libraries on the continent.

Newport also possessed a 'publick school' staffed by young graduates of Harvard and Yale, which, though not a free school in the modern sense, did accept 'many poor children gratis.' It was here that young Henry Alline received his early education, being, as he later put it, 'something forward in learning.'[3] He was taught to read, write, and cipher, and was probably introduced to the traditional classical education of 18th-century Anglo-America. Unfortunately, his formal education ended at the age of 11 with the family's migration to Nova Scotia, and his later writings show little evidence of the mastery of Greek, Latin, and Hebrew which marked an educated man of his time. Alline did, however, gain the basis of what was in his maturity a more than serviceable literary style, and he did so in an educational institution which would stand comparison with any in North America.

But his early education in Newport was scarcely confined to formal schooling. Young Henry had in addition the advantage of growing up in an urban and urbane community. Newport boasted the erudite Ezra Stiles – later president of Yale College – as well as a population which cared about books and learning, revelled in extraordinary displays of conspicuous consumption, and experienced the secular hurly-burly of a great 18th-century international seaport. Although Alline came ultimately to dismiss many of the values and life-styles which he had observed and admired in Newport, this rejection was after a

Nova Scotia experience quite alien to his early years in the city. More-over, however much he came to extol the virtues of other-worldly asceticism, he never did so in an anti-intellectual framework. From Newport, Alline brought to Nova Scotia a commitment to intellectual activity which he was unable to communicate to his contemporaries in the province.

While young Henry was growing up in Newport, developments were taking place in Nova Scotia which would significantly alter his life. The province had been ceded to Britain by the French in 1713, but British settlement was slow because of the presence of sizeable numbers of Acadian French on most of the best lands. The expulsion of these Acadians after the outbreak of the Anglo-French War in 1754 need not be recounted here. Whatever motivated the British and however tragic the affair was, it was this action which made available prize lands upon which the Nova Scotia government could settle loyal British subjects. The richest section was the area around the Minas basin, particularly the Annapolis valley. This region of rolling meadows and naturally cleared intervale land was character-ized by fertile soils and a pleasant temperate climate. Many hillsides were covered with wood, and the sea was at the inhabitant's door (although the basin experienced some of the most extreme tides any-where in the world). The bulk of the Acadians had lived here for generations, and had built substantial earthen dykes to control the tidal water and facilitate spring run-off. The land rich from the sea was sufficient to support the Acadians and large numbers of livestock, and although they did not seem to labour hard, they were prosperous and contented. Even before the expulsion, a number of books and pamphlets available to William Alline and his family stressed the value of the land and the dykes. *A Geographical History of Nova Scotia* published in 1749, for example, noted that the tidal washings 'are very good manure, and help greatly to enrich the Soil, insomuch, that the Land with a little Labour, yields fine Crops of Corn the second year after it is drained, and in a few years more, will produce both Scotch, and several other kinds of Seed Grass. Thus the Farmer is furnished with both Corn and Grazing Land in the marshes and a small part of Upland supplies him with Garden Stuff.'[4] As early as 1756, negotiations were begun in New England for new settlers.

The ebbs and flows of military activity prevented much concrete accomplishment in this regard until October 1758, when Governor Charles Lawrence of Nova Scotia published in New England a proclamation which William Alline and many of his compatriots must have studied extremely carefully. Lawrence announced the opening for settlement of 'upwards of one hundred thousand acres of intervale and plow lands, producing wheat, rye, barley, oats, hemp, flax,' which 'have been cultivated for more than one hundred years past and never fail of crops, nor need manuring,' and one hundred thousand acres of upland 'cleared and stocked with English grass, planted with orchards, gardens.'[5] For many New Englanders like William Alline, who were heads of large families, this announcement was electrifying. New England at this time was experiencing a population explosion in its older and more heavily settled sections – particularly eastern Connecticut, southern Rhode Island, and eastern Massachusetts – which in terms of prevailing agricultural practice and an independent yeoman-farmer ideal made these regions seem over-populated. Men in William Alline's position found it increasingly difficult to assure that sons and daughters would be able to move onto self-supporting farms of their own. The result was, in the 1750s, a steady movement to unsettled lands on the frontiers of America: New York, Pennsylvania, New Hampshire, the northern district of Massachusetts (now Maine), and, of course, Nova Scotia. In many ways, migration to Nova Scotia seemed particularly attractive. The government was offering large grants of free land, as well as promising to pay transportation costs and initial support in the new settlements. Transportation from coastal New England was entirely by water, far more convenient than the hardship of overland movement in the 18th century. And the land was cleared and improved by previous inhabitants, which would make settlement much easier than in the wildernesses of inland North America. William Alline and many others were interested, and desired to know more about the Nova Scotia government's plans for the region.

In answer to many queries, Governor Lawrence in January of 1759 issued another proclamation which offered 100 acres of land to each family head and 50 acres for each additional family member. He assured settlers of representation in a provincial legislative assembly created in 1758 with two representatives from each township, and he promised 'full liberty of conscience ... to persons of all persuasions, Papists excepted.' The proclamation intimated, but did not guarantee, that institutions of local government would be those with which New Englanders were familiar.[6] This interpretation was not entirely true, as the settlers subsequently discovered to their dismay. But for the moment New Englanders were assured, and negotiations opened between land promoters, settlers' agents, and the government. William Alline joined a group of 113 inhabitants of Rhode Island and Connecticut which was granted land for a settlement on the north bank of the Pisiquid River at what was to become Falmouth, in King's County. Although William Alline was probably not himself a farmer, he was undoubtedly as anxious as anyone to guarantee land for his children in an age when land served not only as a means of livelihood but as a basis for social status as well.

Shortly after the Falmouth grant had been seemingly consummated, several upsetting developments occurred. It was discovered that some of the land in question had already been granted by the government in 1736, and formal proceedings were needed to reacquire it from the original grantees. This was largely a technical problem, but it did delay a legal grant to Falmouth until 1761, long after settlement and land distribution had begun. More critical was a severe hurricane which struck the Nova Scotia coast in November of 1759, causing the tides on the Bay of Fundy to rise as much as ten feet above normal. The result was destruction or damage to many of the Acadian dykes. Neither the government in Halifax nor the settlers could ascertain how serious the damage had been, but it undoubtedly contributed to a general feeling of uneasiness on the part of many of the grantees. Moving hundreds of miles to a new community was an enormous gamble, and the Allines could not be sure of either proper title to the land promised them or the advantages of prior improvements. Many grantees, including William Alline, hesitated about taking the final step.

In 1760 the Alline family, 'after a long consultation,' decided finally to emigrate to Nova Scotia.[7] But the understandable delay in making this decision meant that they were not among the first settlers, who arrived in Falmouth on schedule in May of 1760 aboard two government-chartered sloops, the *Sally* and the *Lydia*. The 13 families in this vanguard were naturally concerned about the future of their settlement, particularly in view of the hurricane's damage and the absence of anyone among the arrivals familiar with the dykes. Nevertheless, not all that they found was discouraging. The government had erected a palisade fort for military protection, and a government agent was already on the spot to provide assistance. These first settlers were rewarded for their adventurousness by finding a number of undamaged Acadian buildings which were subsequently distributed in the summer of 1760 to those first arrived in the township.

The Allines' hesitation meant also that the family was not present at Falmouth to assist in the long-familiar actions which New England had institutionalized for the founding of new communities. A series of town meetings held on 9 and 10 June 1760 chose by vote of the adult male inhabitants a moderator (or chairman), a clerk, and a managing committee, and then proceeded to plan distribution of public lands for a commons, a town site, and various religious and educational purposes. Preparations were begun for surveying and inspecting the lands of the township in advance of their distribution to the grantees according to New England custom. A township herdsman was chosen to regulate movement of cattle and other livestock until fencing could be erected, and the cutting of wood was carefully controlled. The settlers took for granted that the government would approve of their actions. The proclamation of 1759 had stated, after all, that Nova Scotia was to have political institutions similar to those in New England; to those familiar by long residence with New England communities, this meant the settling of important local business through democratic discussion and vote in the open meetings. In July the township meeting allocated the standing Acadian buildings, a process in which no Alline participated. Henry Alline and his family must therefore have arrived in Falmouth sometime later in the year, although in time to take part in the distribution of land in the autumn of 1760.

The Falmouth grant of 1759 did not specify the total amount of acreage to be allotted to each grantee, perhaps because it was assumed that the government formula of 100 acres for each head of household and 50 acres for each additional family member would be observed. According to the official grant of 1761, William Alline received an amount exactly coinciding with government policy: 500 acres, 100 for himself, 50 for his wife, and 50 for each of seven children. Despite government propaganda emphasizing the immediate utility of the land, the Alline grant probably included only about 25 acres of readily tillable soil. The remainder would have to be cleared and prepared for use, a task that would consume many hours of labour over a number of years, and which young Henry would supervise. The township made every attempt to assure that each grantee got his fair share of the improved and more promising unimproved land, a standard New England practice. William Alline's land was apparently subsequently discovered to be inferior, and an adjustment was made in 1762.

Along with every other grantee or proprietor in Falmouth, William Alline received a half-acre house lot in a central township plot located across the river from the present town of Windsor. In the 17th century, New Englanders had begun their settlement of the New World in this form of compact, nucleated community, partly because it was familiar to them from England, and partly because it made political-religious functions more accessible to the residents. By the 18th century, however, settlement in New England had become much more scattered, with each inhabitant usually building his house on his own fenced farmland rather than in a central community. In Nova Scotia the initial emphasis was on compact settlement for military reasons rather than out of a sense either of tradition or of purpose. But the insistence meant that the Allines and their fellow settlers were to live together in a community, and would walk or ride to their lands. A continued emphasis upon such compact settlements would have done much to compensate for primitive living conditions and the isolation from the outside world of the townships of the Minas basin. Had the people of Falmouth and her sister townships maintained centralized homesites, a much more active social, cultural, and religious life would have been possible than was the case with individuals scattered on isolated farmlots over an extensive area. Unfortunately, the government of Nova Scotia, which interfered in local affairs in a variety of ways, failed or refused to insist upon nucleated villages. Most settlers, including the Allines, quickly moved to their farmlots, and the social, cultural, and psychological advantages of a sense of community were lost.

The major farm plot of the Allines was a long thin strip situated inland from the Pisiquid River. William Alline drew the location by lot on 15 November 1760. Each proprietor also drew a 'six-acre lot' near the central townsite (probably intended for gardening) and in addition received woodlots as well as dyke lots in the old Acadian section. William Alline did not technically enjoy complete ownership of his land, for he owed to the king a small annual quitrent (which the government of Nova Scotia agreed initially not to collect), and he was forbidden from selling or alienating the land. It was to be returned to the authorities if William did not use it himself. These limitations were undoubtedly not considered of great importance by the settlers in the first years. What mattered was that for those who were 'proprietors' in Falmouth – and apparently all who settled before 1761 were so regarded even if they had not been part of the 1759 agreement with the government – the distribution of land was eminently fair and democratic. One of the major reasons for migration to Nova Scotia had been the difficulty of obtaining land in the settled regions of New England, and the settlers (as was true everywhere in British North America) tended to forget about the limitations placed upon their title to the land. In any case, the Allines and their neighbours, having participated in the process of allocating their own property, could turn with some hope to the years of hardship which would follow.

Nowhere in North America were the early years of new settlement easy ones, and Nova Scotia was no exception. In Falmouth, conditions may have been a bit more trying for those like the Allines who had not arrived in time to share in the allocation of the existing Acadian buildings. For the first winter, and perhaps longer, the Allines apparently lived in a tent, semi-exposed to the elements, including the damp cold and slushy snow of the Nova Scotia season. Housing was not the only difficulty. Food shortages were endemic in the first years of settlement. These were caused by a variety of factors. Sufficient amounts of land were not immediately available for planting, and many, including the Alline family, arrived after the planting season. Few of the settlers brought with them sufficient stocks of seed, and fewer still had any experience with Nova Scotian weather conditions and particularly the growing season, which was considerably shorter than in southern New England. Former urban dwellers such as the Allines must have found adjustment particularly hard. During a food shortage, a run of bad weather could become extremely critical, and Nova Scotia experienced just such a run in the early 1760s.

The settlers at Falmouth did succeed in harvesting 600 tons of hay in 1760, undoubtedly grown on the Acadian dyke lands which were virtually the only part of the township readily available for agriculture. Small plots of vegetables which were planted suffered great damage from bad weather. The provincial government was forced to step in with assistance on a large scale during the winter of 1760–61. The Alline family kept alive on a diet of corn, mackerel, and flour, which provided sustenance but little more. The shortage of food resulted in the consumption of much which should have been retained as seed, and sufficient supplies of seed could not be imported from New England to take up the slack. Beginning in 1761, the settlers in Falmouth managed to clear a good deal of additional land for planting, and although the provincial government continued to provide bounties through 1763, in April of that year it announced the cessation of government assistance. The inhabitants were on their own. Fortunately, by this time local agriculture was prepared to respond to the challenge.

While his parents worried over the housing shortage and the food crisis, young Henry Alline was concerned with other matters. It is not surprising that a city-bred and sensitive adolescent should be impressed less with prosaic difficulties than with more romantic and sensational ones, particularly the Indian menace. In recalling the trails of his early years in Nova Scotia, Henry emphasized that 'it was frequently reported, that the Indians were about rising to destroy us; and many came out among us with their faces painted, and declared that the English should not settle this country.'[8] The young man's understandable fears could scarcely have been allayed by conversations with his family's nearest neighbours, the Payzants. In 1756 the elder Payzant – a Huguenot from Caen who immigrated to Nova Scotia in 1753 – had been massacred by Indians. His wife and children were seized, taken to Quebec, and finally freed only in 1759. The Nova Scotia government settled Mary Payzant and her family in Falmouth as compensation for their losses and sufferings. Young John Payzant, about the same age as Henry Alline and always his closest friend, undoubtedly had many a hair-raising story to tell of his adventures in captivity. Small wonder that Henry 'laid awake many and many an hour, sometimes almost all night listening' and thought when he 'heard the dog bark, or the cattle walking around' that the Indians had come to massacre his family! Alarms about Indians and Acadians continued until well after the signing of the European peace treaty in 1763. The government had some soldiers in the townships, and the local militia was called out on more than one occasion. Though no serious trouble was ever encountered, this hazard was one more pressure upon the new settlers.

Among other hardships in the early years of settlement was the absence in the Minas basin townships of any organized religious or educational activities. Earlier generations of New England settlers had insisted that the founding of new communities could not be undertaken without providing for religious worship and schooling. But the Nova Scotia settlers had not taken such precautions, partly out of their poverty but mainly because such steps were no longer in America considered a prerequisite to settlement. Nevertheless, a population accustomed to the advantages of schools and churches – as most people from New England were – quickly felt their absence. For those like the Allines who had been urban dwellers, the lack of these elements of settled existence was particularly apparent. Young Henry did pick up at least the rudiments of the French language, probably from his friend John Payzant, but he noted with regret that he received no formal schooling after leaving Rhode Island; when he finally decided that he wanted and required more education, he was forced to consider returning to New England to acquire it. Perhaps even more critical was the lack of religious instruction and observance. One of the leaders of the Falmouth community was a former church deacon who may have preached occasionally, but Shubael Dimock was no substitute for a full-time minister. Falmouth built no structure in which religious services could be held during its early years, and religion was preserved only by means such as those employed by the Alline family: regular observance of family prayer, Bible reading, and religious discussions within the home.

The early years of settlement also brought increasing proof that the implicit political promises made to the New England immigrants were not to be honoured. A legislative act which had permitted the settlers to divide their own lands was vetoed by the British government in 1761. Divisions already made, such as that in which William Alline had participated in Falmouth, were to be honoured, but no re-allocations were to be tolerated. Perhaps equally important, regulations introduced by the legislature in 1759 for the city of Halifax turned the selection of local officers (such as overseers of the poor, hog-reeves, surveyors of highways, and fence-viewers) over to the Grand Jury of the provincial Court of General Sessions. By spring of 1761 these Halifax procedures had been extended to King's County, and on 2 April the Grand Jury chose for the townships of Horton, Cornwallis, Falmouth, and East Falmouth (later Newport), surveyors of highways, surveyors of lumber, fence-viewers, and pound-keepers. In November of the same year the appointment of constables was added to the Grand Jury's responsibilities, and in 1762 overseers of the poor were selected the same way. After 1760 the Governor and his Council appointed the key office of dyke commissioner in the townships. Even as a proprietor and voter, William Alline quickly lost the privilege of participating in the selection of most officials who governed him.

The process of discouraging New England town-meeting democracy in Nova Scotia was in full accord with the general position favoured by many enlightened imperial reformers, who saw a great danger to the lauded balance of the British constitution in what seemed to them an over-emphasis in America on the democratic will of the people. William Douglass in 1747 advocated the policy followed in Nova Scotia in his *A Summary, Historical and Political, of the First Planting, Progressive Improvements, and Present State of the British Settlements in North America*; Douglass was a close friend of Governor Jonathan Belcher of Massachusetts, father of the Jonathan Belcher who governed Nova Scotia during much of the township controversy. For settlers like William Alline, subtle constitutional adjustments were direct threats to their prerogatives as guaranteed by the province, particularly when local government was under attack. Most of the New England population in Nova Scotia cared far more about local than central government. Local government was more immediate to them and concerned with affairs that mattered. Beginning in 1761, William Alline could vote to send Falmouth's two representatives to the provincial assembly which met at Halifax; he could even become a candidate. But such delegates were unpaid, and the cost in time and money of travelling to and living in Halifax put provincial office-holding beyond the reach of the average settler. Moreover, who could worry about larger issues when faced with the more immediate ones of surviving? Not surprisingly, Falmouth persistently selected outsiders to represent it in Halifax. In the pre-revolutionary period only three individuals were elected to represent Falmouth: Henry Denny Denson, Isaac Deschamps, and Edward York. Denson and Deschamps were both Halifax-connected landholders in Falmouth, and only York (whose seat was declared vacant in 1775 for non-attendance) was a New Englander. William Alline, his neighbours, and their sons ultimately paid for their lack of concern with provincial affairs. The assembly in which they could have had a sizeable voice took the lead in the total abolition of township democracy.

New England settlers gradually became aware that political developments were running against their interests. In 1762 the citizens of Liverpool protested that removal of the 'right and authority ... to nominate and appoint men among us to be our committee and to do other offices that the Town may want' was an encroachment 'in our Freedom and Liberty and depriving us of a privilege that belongs to no body of people but ourselves.'⁹ In 1763 the inhabitants of King's County (in which the Allines resided) submitted a similar petition to the British government protesting the failure of the Nova Scotia authorities to incorporate their townships, their inability to redivide their lands, and their lack of power to select their own officers and transact local affairs. The New Englanders got some support for their complaints from members of the provincial executive, but the provincial assembly, probably fearful of threats to its own power, authority, and prerogatives which might result from strong local government, refused to permit the townships to do much more than maintain their own poor.

Despite physical hardship, the absence of the amenities of civilization, and unhappiness with political developments, by the beginning of 1764 the Allines and their neighbours were over the initial difficulties of founding a new community. A census of 1763 recorded nearly

80 families (just over 350 persons) in the township of Falmouth; most of those not prepared to endure privation had by now retreated to New England. The period of day-to-day crisis was over, and the obstacles of initial organization, housing, food, and threats of violence familiar to the Allines had been surmounted. After 1764 the New England settlements of the Minas basin moved into a period of consolidation and relative stability which would be terminated only with the outbreak of the American Revolution. For Henry Alline, these years after 1764 were ones of great importance, for it was in this period that he passed through adolescence to manhood. Probably too young to appreciate just how uncertain life actually was in the days of early settlement, his clearest memories were of this later period. The township in which he lived remained on the periphery of civilization and experienced further limitations of local control; cultural and religious disabilities were not much improved. Nevertheless, peace and stability did greatly improve material living conditions for most New Englanders who remained in Nova Scotia, and life in the rural townships did develop a form and pattern of its own. Henry came to feel a part of this 'country life,' but he was never entirely comfortable in it.

The Allines settled into a regular rhythm and routine based upon agrarian activities. Like most of their neighbours, they depended on family agriculture for survival. Henry's older brother William moved off onto a farmstead of his own, and his father operated a small grain mill. This left Henry, as the eldest son living at home, to supervise farming operations on the family's holdings, and he worked long hours in the fields. As time went on, the family came to rely more and more upon Henry, and by the eve of the American Revolution he was effectual head of the household. His parents, by this time in their sixties, undoubtedly followed the long-standing New England tradition of expecting Henry to remain at home and provide for their old age in return for the right to inherit the family property upon their death. Up to the point when he began his evangelical career, Henry apparently accepted this expectation, which meant, among other things, that he deferred any thoughts of marriage. This postponement was common not only in New England but in most agrarian societies.

The daily routine was least demanding upon Henry in the winter months, particularly between December and April, when snow covered the ground. During this time farmers kept busy with hunting and lumbering, the latter providing many with the only cash crop. Winter was the season when Henry was best able to pursue a program of reading and study. In the early spring, he would have to clear trees and brush from land not yet ready for cultivation. May was for plowing, and by the end of the month fields were sown and crops planted. Despite the late start, everything grew rapidly. At the close of the June planting season, Henry could turn to fishing in local waters and to clearing more land. Berrying was an important activity during July and August, and fruit from local orchards had to be picked. The hay harvest, critical for maintaining the cattle and horses kept by each settler, was taken in at the end of August. September, October, and early November were harvest months, and by late November winter was again setting in. Livestock, of course, had to be fed and looked after throughout the year, and buildings needed constant attention. In the annual cycle an industrious farmer had little opportunity for prolonged leisure and the cultivation of the mind.

Unlike the New England settlements on the west and south coasts of Nova Scotia, which were basically fishing communities with small-scale farming as a supplement, those in the Minas basin consisted mainly of family farms operating on a subsistence basis, with the inhabitants producing for themselves most of the essentials of life. Hard money and currency were always in short supply in Nova Scotia. The Anglican missionary Joseph Bennett wrote to England in 1767 that

'You never knew so great a scarcity of money as prevails in this province ... a man with great difficulties can get Cash for a Sterling bill.'[10] Permanent servants or even temporary hired help were difficult and expensive to obtain, which was why the family unit was so important. What little surplus was produced was generally traded with New England, which had far better transportation links with the townships than did Halifax. For the Allines, overland ties with Halifax consisted as late as 1768 only of treacherous footpaths beyond Windsor. As one official of the government in 1766 described the situation:

At present although several Paths have been cut to some of the Settlements; yet none but that to Windsor have been so far compleated, as to admit of Carriages, which is yet in an imperfect State, nor is any other passable for Horses without Difficulty (that to Annapolis excepted) on account of the Swamps and Rivers over which there are no Bridges; so that they may be deemed a Direction to the foot Travellers only.[11]

The government made pious pronouncements about improving roads, but lacked financial resources, which neither appeals to the British government nor local lotteries supplied. Most communication with the outside world on the part of farmers in the Minas townships, therefore, was by sea through the agency of Yankee sea captains and traders. Despite a subsistence economy, Henry Alline and his family were able to live reasonably comfortably, though scarcely in luxury. The woods contained a good supply of game, particularly deer and wild fowl, and the rivers and bays teemed with fish and shellfish. Wild berries and fruit were available in season. The Allines' diet could be rich and varied, at least during the summer and autumn. In an era before the introduction of modern cooking techniques and preservation facilities, the winter and spring menu was considerably more limited. At this time, the presence of fresh meat on the table frequently meant the killing of much-valued livestock, and all settlers lived largely on pickled pork, salted fish, dried corn, and various root vegetables. Nevertheless, European visitors to Nova Scotia were always impressed with the relative abundance of food, and accounts of diet which remain indicate that, even in the winter months, malnutrition was caused less by food shortages than by lack of variety and proper balance in the diet. These were universal problems.

Many of the necessities of life beyond foodstuffs were homemade, and the settlers lived simply. Henry's mother and sisters undoubtedly spun, wove, and dyed their own cloth, and made their own candles, soap, starch, and yeast. Most settlers dressed in homespun clothes during the week, the men in checked shorts, breeches or long trousers, the women in woolseys and jackets. The high cost of stays (corsets) made these items of feminine apparel uncommon despite their current fashionableness elsewhere. On the Sabbath, those who attended worship services dressed in their finest linen and cloth. The men in the Alline family wore their hair in a queue; the women tied theirs at the neck during the week and piled it high on their heads for special occasions. In the summer most rural Nova Scotians went barefoot much of the time.

The Allines eventually moved out of their temporary shelter into more permanent accommodations, which Henry would certainly have helped to build. Their square wooden house, like those of most of their neighbours, probably had a centre chimney (with fireplaces for each downstairs room) and a good many sashed windows. Since glass was a rare and expensive commodity, windows were covered with oiled paper instead. The houses would usually contain a full cellar, which was used to store root crops. Nova Scotia architecture reminded observers of rural New England, its houses covered with unpainted clapboarding on the side walls and planked shingle on the roof. Interior decoration was fairly simple and furnishings were minimal. Most farms consisted of a dwelling house and a number of out-buildings, the prominent one being the barn, a wooden structure usually clapboarded and shingled, with a second floor for storing hay and corn. Livestock was housed in partitioned compartments on the first floor, which had an entrance sufficiently large to permit a loaded wagon to enter.

Although the life lived by Henry Alline and his family in early rural Nova Scotia was relatively unsophisticated and plain, like most settlers from New England they retained certain of the civilized amenities from their former homes. Travellers commented on the degree to which the Sabbath was observed – despite a relative lack of organized religion – and on the religious upbringing given to most children, who were taught 'a right notion of religion, and the great duty they owe to God and their parents.'[12] This was certainly the pattern in the Alline household. Little profanity was heard in the New England townships, except perhaps from outsiders like Colonel Henry Denny Denson, about whom the Falmouth settlers complained in 1763 for foul and abusive language. At the same time that children were brought up to respect their parents, to speak politely, and to 'move the hat and foot on passing their superiors,' New England rural society in Nova Scotia was far more democratic and unpretentious than that in England. As in most households, the entire Alline family ate at a single table at the same time, and they maintained few social distinctions with their neighbours, everyone being called 'Misters and Sirs, and their maidens ... Misses.'[13]

However much the struggle for existence was hard and perpetual, country life was not all work and toil. Settlers met communally for a variety of activities such as weddings and barn-raisings, with 'frolicks' and parties quite common among the young of both sexes, especially in the winter months. In Falmouth, Henry Alline was a leader of the young people in his community, and for many years was at the centre of youthful amusements. He attended a constant round of parties and dances which featured a fiddler, songs, and games. After the mid 1760s he could attend an annual fair at Windsor, where prizes were awarded for the best local produce and where horse racing was a special feature. Since Nova Scotian horses were small and bred less as draft animals than for riding, the races were probably reasonably stirring. Amusements in early rural Nova Scotia were simple by modern standards, but they helped the population to relieve the drudgery and boredom of the daily routine.

The Annapolis valley was not the only rural area in Nova Scotia, and conditions were not identical everywhere. The fishing communities to the south and west contained more single men and did not place so much emphasis on family life; they tended to be less stable and prosperous than a township like Falmouth. The Cumberland settlements on the northern neck contained a high percentage of newer immigrants from Europe, and had their own traditions. But all rural areas had in common a sense of distinctiveness from Nova Scotia's one urban centre, Halifax. In 1774, according to a traveller, Halifax was a town 'pleasantly situated on the west-side of the harbour ... above a mile in length and three or four streets broad in some parts; it contains upwards of six thousand inhabitants.' Halifax had the king's 'only dockyard in North America' and 'large and convenient barracks for above a thousand men.'[14] Besides housing the military establishment, Halifax contained the nerve-centres of government, published the province's only newspapers, and was the commercial and manufacturing centre. For the rural Nova Scotian, Halifax was not only the source of political authority, but, with its taverns, theatres, brothels, and hard-living military men, it was Sodom and Gomorrah as well.

All Nova Scotia society was characterized by the heavy consumption of alcoholic beverages, with rum the preferred drink. But rural areas did not institutionalize dissipation in the same way as Halifax. Many farmers seem to have insisted upon a glass immediately upon rising in the morning, and some spent their evenings in local taverns (usually kept by widowed women), drinking and arguing. Most settlers may have manufactured their own liquor, especially the fabled 'spruce beer' made by boiling bark and molasses, then allowing the mixture to ferment. But as early as 1760, Halifax was said to have 'upwards of 100 licensed houses, and perhaps as many more which retail spirituous liquors without license; so that the business of one-half of the town is to sell rum, and of the other half to drink it.'[15] Rural Nova Scotians may have 'frolicked,' but they did not attend the 'Play-House ... the Palace of Asmodeus, the Seat of Lewdness, the Nursery of Debauchery.' One critic in 1770 argued that 'For my part I am of Opinion that a Christian cannot with a safer Conscience enter into the Playhouse than into a Brothel.'[16] Henry Alline came ultimately to reject liquor even in moderation and innocent parties as 'useless earthly pleasures and vanities,' and not surprisingly, the sinfulness of Halifax was so beyond his comprehension that he never felt comfortable in the city.

Halifax's distinctive reputation in the eyes of rural settlers was added to by its undoubted political domination. In the years up to 1765 the inhabitants of the Minas basin continued quietly to hold town meetings and transact local business. But in that year a new township act passed by the legislature took the power of appointment from the Grand Jury and gave it to the justices of the Court (Halifax appointees), who were to act upon nominations from the Grand Jury. This had the effect of further reducing the control over local affairs by the inhabitants. The same year saw a reduction of representation in the assembly from two to one per township. The reason given for this action – the increasing size and unwieldiness of the legislative body – may have been legitimate, but again the countryside found its political position altered unilaterally. As if to demonstrate a conviction that the assembly was not 'their' ruling body – a feeling aided by difficulties of travel and communication – the settlers continued to elect prominent Haligonians and government officials to represent them. Although almost all power had after 1765 been stripped from the townships, Henry Alline could have attended local meetings until 1770, when activities from these bodies suggesting support for the rebels in New England led the Halifax government to forbid all local assemblies.

The Alline family was not politically active either before or after the effectual ending of town meeting democracy in Nova Scotia, and Henry came of political age only after local political authority had been completely emasculated. He served one term as local constable when appointed by the Court of General Sessions, but the office of constable – who kept the peace and enforced local regulations – was considered an onerous one. Being constable was a duty, not an honour. Henry quite obviously was an energetic young man. He worked long hours to help support his family, and still had the vigour both to seek self-improvement through education and to lead the young people of his community in a variety of harmless amusements. Any inclination which he may have had to seek an outlet for his extraordinary energy in government and politics was unquestionably stifled by the closed system of local and provincial politics in effect in early Nova Scotia.

The rulers of the province were in the main correct in assuming that the absence of harsh financial levies upon the population would keep it relatively apathetic, to whatever extent the settlers were governed by a political system with which they were not in favour and which they did not control. Nova Scotia had no direct taxation, and indirect taxes were exacted mainly on luxury goods and rums. The government made no concerted effort to collect quitrents which were due it, and most settlers had no reason to complain of the corruption in Halifax, since not they but the British treasury was being systematically bilked. Young men with energy could always return to New England or marry and acquire their own property; raising a family in rural Nova Scotia would keep anyone extremely busy. Henry Alline had acquiesced in responsibilities which made it difficult for him to follow either of these paths. He needed an outlet, but the system did not permit or encourage a bright young man from the backcountry without connections to enter politics and become involved in government. Part of the guilt he felt about his participation in community amusements like dances and parties was undoubtedly a result of his recognition that he was engaged in non-constructive activities. Not surprisingly, therefore, Henry increasingly turned his attention inward toward concern for his spiritual condition.

In a quest for spiritual truth in rural Nova Scotia before 1775, Henry Alline could expect little assistance from formal religious institutions. The situation that faced him in Falmouth was, if anything, worse than elsewhere in the province. The achievement of economic stability after 1764 made it possible for some of the New England townships in Nova Scotia to obtain regular ministers, frequently university-trained men from New England, but these men were not prepared to accept primitive living conditions. They expected regular salaries and prerequisites to maintain themselves and their families in at least minimum comfort. Most ministers remained only a short time in Nova Scotia, and their pastorates were filled with continual conflicts with their congregations over finances. The neighbouring communities of Cornwallis and Granville both enjoyed the ministrations of two of the more persistent New England pastors. But though Benajah Phelps and Arzareleah Morse remained in faithful service to their congregations until after the outbreak of the American Revolution, when their moral support of the rebels caused them difficulty, they did not seem at all anxious to bring religion to the township of Falmouth, which had no settled minister of any denomination.

Although the Allines and most inhabitants of Falmouth were by upbringing New England Puritans, they would probably have been responsive to almost anyone who offered his assistance. James Murdoch, an Irish Presbyterian minister at nearby Horton after 1767, apparently made no efforts to assist Falmouth in its distress. The Church of England tried to do something, however, and after 1762 the Minas region was served by Joseph Bennett, an Anglican missionary. Bennett, who was paid by the Society for the Propagation of the Gospel in Foreign Parts (known as the SPG) in England, was not forced to seek local financial support, but his mission area was enormous and he could devote little time to Falmouth. The need was so great, however, that despite New England conviction that Anglicanism was exceeded in perfidy and heresy only by Roman Catholicism, Bennett was tolerated as a man of God as an alternative to no minister at all. Although the Church of England was technically the established church of the province, few inhabitants were aware of this and the Anglicans did not much press the point in this period. For several years in the late 1760s, Newport – the village adjacent to Falmouth – enjoyed the services of John Sutton, a Baptist minister from New Jersey. But Sutton left in 1769, and Joseph Bennett opined 'I really think I shall never see another dissenting minister settled in Either of them towns [Falmouth and Newport] more.'[17] Most of the residents would probably have despairingly agreed.

In the absence of pastoral counselling, young Henry Alline was placed upon his own resources in his search for spiritual truth. Given the shortage of books and other instruments of culture in the Falmouth area, religious self-education was no mean task. He may have had an opportunity to read the *Halifax Gazette*, the province's only newspaper for most of the period, but he undoubtedly found in its pages no answers to the religious questions he was asking. Few printed works made their way to the Annapolis valley, and the planning of a rational reading program was impossible. All Henry could do was to devour voraciously whatever came to hand – a few works of devotional literature – and to rely upon his Bible.

Henry Alline undoubtedly had a psychological disposition toward the brand of religious experience which he ultimately espoused and promoted – a personal religion of the heart with tendencies toward mysticism and against authority – but political, social, cultural, and religious circumstances in the Minas basin certainly contributed to this inclination. Inexperienced as he was in formal and communal religious activity, it was not surprising that he would minimize formalism in his own teaching. Excluded as he must have felt from political activity in his spiritually formative years, it was understandable that he would seek in religion an alternative to political involvement and ultimately reject secular government as a worthwhile enterprise for himself and others. Exposed on the one hand to heavy drinking and on the other to harmlessly unconstructive amusements, he developed an ethic which stressed spiritual asceticism and viewed such activities as worthless. Denied the opportunity to marry by family circumstances and general custom, he committed himself to Christ. Unable to develop his intellectual position through exposure to the full range of human thinking, he drew heavily on the very limited resources at his disposal and found the results coincided with his own inclinations. Alline's spiritual experiences and his religious ethic were deeply conditioned by his environment. His dissatisfactions may have been shared by other rural Nova Scotians, but he almost alone had both the sensitiveness and the energy not only to reject the world in which he lived but to offer a positive alternative for himself and his neighbours.

2

Redeeming Love Broke into My Soul

The ultimate result of Henry Alline's evangelical career was to undermine and virtually destroy the Puritan orthodoxy which his family and most of their fellow New Englanders had brought with them to Nova Scotia. Despite his subsequent attacks on Calvinistic doctrine and on the practices of the Puritan churches, however, the process by which Alline achieved personal spiritual truth was entirely within the bounds of the Puritan tradition. Indeed, Alline's conversion experiences, which he recorded at length as part of his legacy to the world, were so typical of New England Puritanism that his account of them seems almost stereotyped. If anything out of the ordinary was present in Alline's relation of his conversion, it was in terms of length (from age 8 to age 26) and intensity rather than in configuration. Alline's conversion followed closely the pattern set forth by Puritan theologians over a period of several centuries and epitomized by hundreds of individual Puritans detailing their own experiences.

That Alline should record the major event of his life in almost stereotyped terms might be expected. Although the Minas basin may have been deficient in its formal religious activity, it had large numbers of residents who had been exposed to and indeed participated in the greatest of all North American explosions of evangelical pietism, the Great Awakening of the 1740s in New England. Most of the Yankee settlers in Nova Scotia came from areas which had been heavily affected by the Awakening – especially eastern Massachusetts, coastal Rhode Island, and eastern Connecticut. A strong correlation existed between those regions experiencing the land shortages which produced emigration to new communities and areas responding favourably to the phenomenon of revivalism. To whatever extent the Awakening in New England was or was not caused by socio-economic conditions, it did produce a renewed interest in the nature of personal conversion – in pietistic terms – an interest which was brought to Nova Scotia.

One of the results of this new concern was the publication or re-printing of the spiritual experiences of many a Puritan pietist. Among the most popular of these works was the spiritual diary of the Indian missionary David Brainerd, which was edited by Jonathan Edwards (one of the high priests of the New England revival) and which served countless individuals as a model both for the Christian experience and for the Christian life. The diary of Brainerd, the journals of the Anglican evangelist George Whitefield, and a variety of accounts of other Puritans (such as John Bunyan) whose spiritual experiences were considered edifying and uplifting became best-sellers in 18th-century America. Nova Scotia experienced a shortage of more abstruse doctrinal works, but these less technical and highly popular books were undoubtedly brought to Nova Scotia along with family Bibles by many of the New England settlers. They were available for study to young Henry Alline, who later recorded, 'I read of many experiences and accounts of a work of grace in the souls of others.'[1] These popular devotional works made it fashionable for those with pietistic leanings to keep some sort of spiritual 'diary,' and Henry Alline was no exception. Using such 'accounts' – which were invariably couched in the standard Puritan conversion idiom – as a model and inspiration for explaining his own conversion, Alline's narrative naturally echoed that of others.

New England Puritanism, although basically Calvinistic, had modified and refined the teachings of the great Geneva reformer in a variety of ways. Subtle doctrinal matters ultimately became of concern to Henry Alline, particularly toward the end of his career, but at this formative stage of his life they were considerably less important. Although, as he noted, he 'did read and study much,' soon attaining 'a great theory of religion for one of my age,' what really concerned young Alline was his personal relationship with God.[2] In a way, doctrinal subtleties did not matter here. Puritans within a great range of theological positions could agree on this point, and had developed a map of the 'route from sin to holiness and explained the way God carried a saint along it.'[3] Underlying this chart were any number of theological assumptions and hidden disagreements, but one did not need to comprehend or acquiesce in theological fine points to accept the basic stages outlined in many writings and exemplified in the various 'accounts of a work of grace.' Learned Puritan divines worked out the details in their studies and argued over them in assemblies; what the average individual needed were the directions, which became standardized.

Not all Puritans were agreed on the exact number of the stages on the road to conversion but five can readily be identified. First came Christian knowledge, based upon church attendance, family worship, and catechism. Here one came to understand intellectually what God's word was, and once this understanding was achieved, the individual could then be brought – by God – to an awareness of the distinctions between good and evil. This awareness merged imperceptibly into the second stage, which Puritans called 'conviction.' Here the individual 'perceived his helpless and hopeless condition and despaired of salvation.'[4] Conviction was hardly synonymous with salvation; many never got beyond this 'legal fear.' But to some (in Calvinistic terms the 'elect'), God gave a will and desire to believe in Him that was usually labelled 'grace.' This third stage did not complete the conversion process. The individual soon found that his soul began to doubt and despair of having actually experienced saving faith, and he engaged in a prolonged struggle against his fears of insufficiency. The fourth stage of combat against doubt never really ended, but eventually the true saint would triumph over his despair and achieve some sense of personal assurance, the fifth and final step in the conversion process.

Henry Alline described the conversion process in terms consistent with the above analysis in *Two Mites Cast into the Offering of God*. With many Puritans Alline held that 'although the work of conversion is instantaneous, yet the work of conviction may be gradual.' The question of which stage was instantaneous and which prolonged was one as old as Puritanism. For orthodox Puritans total assurance was never achieved, since the absence of continuing doubt demonstrated self-delusion rather than genuine faith. One of the criticisms later levied against Henry Alline and his followers was that they were too certain, too spiritually arrogant, and hence not true saints. But as Alline's diary indicates, personal doubts did continue, however much his actions may sometimes have belied them. Knowledge, conviction, grace (or saving faith), combat, and assurance: these were the stages through which Puritans passed on their way to holiness and sainthood, and Henry Alline's conversion was no exception.

Despite attacks on Calvinism in his account of his spiritual struggles, Alline thus chose, either consciously or unconsciously, to present his experiences in standard Puritan terms. The account in his *Journal* begins with emphasis on his early acquisition of Christian knowledge, the first step on the road to salvation, which quickly merged into evidences of conviction. William and Rebeccah Alline gave him 'an early instruction in the principles of the christian religion,' and he was 'very early moved upon by the spirit of God, though I knew not then what ailed me.' When he was about eight years old, a thunderstorm raised in him concern for death and hell, and that night in bed he began to pray in a serious fashion, though previously he had been taught only 'to repeat a number of words, as I did my lesson at school.' At this point he 'began to examine and study' what he read and was taught in his catechism and he feared God's wrath, for 'I thought myself in great danger, and often, when writing at school would so ponder on my miserable condition, that I could scarcely keep my distress concealed.' From the age of nine, young Alline 'began to read much in the books I could understand, and studied much to find out how to get in favour with the great invisible God.' He attended meetings 'almost every Sabbath' but got little spiritual satisfaction.[5] Even before his family's move to Nova Scotia, therefore, Henry had passed through the first two steps toward conversion. He had reached the stage of attained Christian knowledge, and had recognized his own helplessness in the face of his Creator. His position was probably fairly similar to that of a good many Yankee immigrants to the frontier. Unlike most of his neighbours, however, Henry Alline did not permit the rough way of life in his new home to arrest permanently his spiritual pilgrimage.

In Nova Scotia, the pursuit of Christian knowledge and of an understanding of good and evil continued for young Henry. But like all good Puritans, he found that study and prayer were not enough to gain 'some insight in this infinite mystery.' By the age of 17, he was 'now very moral' in his life but 'found no rest of conscience' in this. As he noted, 'I flattered myself that if I did not get drunk, nor curse, nor swear, there would be no sin in frolicking and carnal mirth, and I thought God would indulge young people with some (what I called simple or civil) recreation.' Attempts to 'break off from bad company' when under temporary distress did not work, and 'the amusements of the time would soon make me be as wild as before.' Alline had reached the point beyond moral life (the so-called 'covenant of works'), but had obviously not experienced the infusion of God's grace. There were signs of change, however, although in his account Alline continually berates himself for his hypocrisy. He was 'the chief contriver and ringleader of the frolicks,' but at heart he was uneasy and 'would act the hypocrite and feign a merry heart.' His parents warned him of the results of continued surrender to 'carnal passions,' but neither their advice nor constant discussion of the 'disputed points' of religion 'such as election, reprobation, resurrection, baptism' did much good.

These, Alline remembered, only 'increased my distress, for I thought I could deceive the very elect.'[6] Such self-deprecation need not be taken strictly at face value, of course, since this was all part of the Puritan process of introspection leading to the acquisition of saving grace.

The first sign of grace came to Alline when he was about 20 years of age. While walking alone at night, he was suddenly 'surrounded with an uncommon light; it seemed like a blaze of fire.' For almost a minute he saw thousands of 'devils and damned spirits,' and realized that he had no way to combat them, since he had wilfully rejected God's grace and mercy. For half an hour he stood trembling, eyes downcast, convinced that he was lost and justly condemned. When he raised his eyes, he saw 'a large blaze of light in the shape of a circle, with that side next to me open as though it yawned after me, and as it drew very nigh me, it closed up in a small compass, then broke out in small sparkles, and vanished away.' Writing years after the event, Alline postulated that the light 'was one of the common phenomena of nature, such as exhaled vapours or nitre, that had gathered in the air.' But this did not really matter, he argued, because 'it was not the less alarming to me; for I believe it was really designed by God as an alarming means, as much as if it was a miracle sent to me in particular.'[7] Although this statement can be taken to mean that Alline was willing to accept a natural explanation for his vision, it is not quite as 'scientific' as it might sound. Alline, like most Puritans, believed that God acted through natural phenomena, and in later years he adopted a good deal of nature mysticism which he learned from the Anglican writer William Law's exposition of the theosophy of Jacob Boehme.

The state of Alline's emotions at this point can best be appreciated in terms of his next experience. Following these initial 'visions' he determined to beg God for mercy and redeeming love. He returned to his home and the privacy of his bedroom. But, he recorded:

I had not been long in the room, before there was represented to my view a beautiful woman (one whom I had seen before, but had no great acquaintance with) and the happiness that I thought I might enjoy with her stole away my affections from thinking much of God or my state. The devil told me that I need not commit any sin for to enjoy her; that I might marry her, which was lawful: yea, I so acquiesced in the temptation, that my affections were after her, and she appeared the most beautiful object that ever I beheld. My passions were so inflamed with the prospect, that I thought I would not omit the first opportunity to go see her and propose marriage to her. I thought I would be the happiest man on earth, if I might but have her for a companion for life.

A psychiatrist would have little difficulty in explaining the significance of this vision, with its obvious sexual overtones. His unmarried state was clearly on Alline's mind at this point, and undoubtedly explains the form which temptation took. He realized his state of mind himself, writing that the vision indicated 'the subtilty of that grand adversary, who might by this temptation have proved my eternal ruin, if God had not interposed." In tried and true Puritan fashion, he had moved beyond the stage of saving faith into that of spiritual combat. He was 'not only made to see the temptation, but likewise to detest it from my very heart, and enabled to withstand it.'[8]

The next few years were for Henry Alline a continual period of distress and uncertainty. 'Wherever I went, or whatever I did, night or day, I was groaning under a load of guilt and darkness, praying and crying continually for mercy.' He remained convinced that he 'had nothing saving' in his heart, and he most feared 'getting back into my former state of security, so as wholly to forget my lost and undone condition.' While visiting some friends, he was disturbed by their mocking of the 'New-Lights' (those awakened by the earlier New England revivals), but though he believed that such an awakening was the work of God, he lacked 'the power to speak in behalf of it.'[9]

Final assurance of conversion came for Alline on 26 March 1775. It was a Sunday, but Falmouth – as usual – had 'no preaching.' So Henry went wandering in the fields, where he was again struck with his own insufficiency and unimportance in the face of God. Returning to the house, he sank into a chair asking 'Will God have mercy upon me, or must I sink forever?' By chance he picked up an old Bible and turned to the 38th Psalm ('O Lord, rebuke me not in thy wrath: neither chasten me in thy hot displeasure'), which 'took hold of me with such power, that it seemed to go through my whole soul, and read therein every thought of my heart, and raised my soul with groans and earnest cries to God, so that it seemed as if God was praying in, with, and for me.' As a result of this experience and continual prayers, he arrived at 'that instant of time when I gave up all to him, to do with me, as he pleased, and was willing that God should reign in me and rule over me at his pleasure.' Suddenly, he recorded, 'redeeming love broke into my soul with repeated scriptures with such power, that my whole soul seemed to be melted down with love.'

Half an hour later, Henry felt a call to 'labour in the ministry and ... preach the gospel.' This experience led to another long period (over a year) of uncertainty and inner debate over the validity of his ministerial call, but it was subsequent to and quite apart from the achievement of assurance conversion. Indeed, Alline admitted, 'I lived a considerable time without any distressing doubts.'[10] Although these ultimately returned, they were henceforth always surmountable. After 26 March 1775 Henry Alline considered himself a converted man, and acted accordingly.

Despite the traditional nature of his conversion experience, Alline was tending to move in a direction away from Puritan theological orthodoxy. To a great extent this tendency resulted from his lengthy internal conflict over his ministerial call, and from political developments in Nova Scotia at this time which would make it impossible for him to follow standard New England procedure for ministerial qualification. But inherent in his personal conversion experience and in the external circumstances of his life in Newport and Nova Scotia were other factors which undermined his traditional Puritan upbringing and values. In his subsequent account of his conversion, Alline emphasized the extent to which his personal experiences deviated from what he had been taught in formal religious instruction. How much of this was *ex post facto* analysis is impossible to ascertain, but it is probably true that Alline at the time of his conversion did uncover what he considered to be discrepancies between 'orthodoxy' as he had been taught it and his own experiences. He was particularly concerned about what he considered to be the failure of traditional Puritanism to emphasize the need for the 'new birth.' But he also objected to the orthodox Calvinistic picture of a vengeful and retributive rather than a loving God, and to the insistence on the doctrine of preordained election of the saints, which underlined the inability of man to act for his own salvation.

These doubts may seem paradoxical for one who was undergoing a traditional Puritan conversion experience, but no paradox really exists. Alline's *experiences* were entirely within the framework of orthodoxy; it was the *conclusions* he drew from them which were not. The inconsistency came about largely because he had not received a fair exposure to and a full understanding of the complex doctrine which was New England Puritanism. For this he could not really be blamed; he had left Rhode Island at an early age – taking away an incomplete view in any case – and had little opportunity for further expansion of his understanding of doctrinal complexities in Nova

Scotia. Moreover, New England Puritanism, always an uneasy attempt to maintain in tension a host of seemingly contradictory concepts and tendencies, had never been a monolithic 'orthodoxy.' In his formative years, no one attempted to explain to Henry Alline how his personal doubts could be reconciled with acceptable Puritan doctrine, and by the time someone undertook this task, his position had hardened far beyond the point where it was reconcilable. Indeed, particularly in the crucial period of his conversion and debate over his call to preach – when Alline was still well within the bounds of New England orthodoxy – all aspects of his personal experience had the tendency to reinforce his ultimate decision to break with traditional Puritanism as he understood it.

Alline's contact with influences which eroded his commitment to New England Puritanism may have begun while his family was still in Rhode Island. Here the Allines frequently attended the Congregational church of which Ezra Stiles was the pastor. Stiles was a learned and urbane man, but his intellectual achievements – which were many – were hardly designed to appeal to the young Henry Alline. A Stiles sermon, packed with erudition and doctrinal subtleties, was not, as Alline commented, 'adapted to the capacity of children,' and not 'tell them in plain words, that they must be born again by the spirit of God, and that they must feel and know this new birth each one for himself.'[11] Such emphasis could hardly be expected of Ezra Stiles, whose father had been one of the principal Connecticut opponents of the Great Awakening, and who himself had been a student at Yale when that university was purged of pietistic elements. But if Alline did not learn about the new birth from Stiles, he may have picked up some of the Newport minister's other views. In intellectual approach, Stiles was a rationalist, and although this would not have appealed to the young Henry Alline, the Newporter's distaste for the Calvinistic view of the depravity of man may have made some impact. So too there might have been an appeal in some of Stiles's ecumenical spirit and scepticism about the value of rigid rules of church practice.

Whatever else Ezra Stiles may have been, he was certainly a full-fledged member of the New England Puritan establishment, and one of its finest products. After leaving Newport, Henry Alline had no further opportunity for exposure to such an individual. In Nova Scotia, Alline's principal ecclesiastical contacts were with those who had either consciously rejected the Puritan establishment or whose religious position was completely outside it. Separate Congregationalists, Baptists, Quakers, and Anglicans composed the major religious forces in the Minas township population, and all of these different traditions may have played a role in Alline's religious development.

Perhaps the most important of these anti-Puritan influences was provided by the Separate Congregationalists, or 'Separates,' as they were usually known. These were New England colonists who had been strongly influenced and frequently converted during the heyday of the Great Awakening in the early 1740s. Like Alline, they tended to emphasize the importance of an intensely emotional conversion experience and the necessity for the 'new birth.' For much of the Puritan establishment in New England, and especially in Connecticut (where traditional Calvinism was extremely powerful and churches carefully regulated from above), these pietistic converts seemed far too radical. Such extremists criticized their ministers for not being converted (in the intense sense that they had been), demanded that the churches be purged of those under the 'covenant of works,' and insisted that the sacraments of the churches – communion and baptism – be restricted to those who met their conception of true saints. Despite the large numbers of pietists, especially in eastern Connecticut, the Puritan establishment in church and state of that colony was able to force out those 'radicals' who did not willingly separate from it. The 'Separates' proceeded to organize their own churches and fight a bitter campaign against the establishment, which persecuted them in a variety of open and subtle ways. Eastern Connecticut was not only the centre of the Separates but also a region of severe land hunger and shortages, and, not surprisingly, large numbers of these anti-establishment Puritans, who considered themselves more orthodox than the churches they had abandoned, came to Nova Scotia.

In Henry Alline's Falmouth, one of the early leaders of the community was Shubael Dimock, formerly deacon of the Separate Church of Mansfield, Connecticut. Dimock had suffered at the hands of the Standing Order, as Separates referred to the Connecticut establishment, and his treatment was a major factor in his decision to emigrate to Nova Scotia, where liberty of conscience had been promised by the government. In Falmouth he preached to a small number of settlers, perhaps including the Alline family, before moving across the river to Newport. Another leading Separate was Daniel Hovey of Horton, father of several Falmouth grantees. Hovey early tested the sincerity of the government's promises of religious liberty. He was arrested and charged by the county Quarter Sessions in 1761 for 'uttering certain scandalous words and expressions tending to stir up sedition in the minds of His Majesty's subjects,' and for undertaking to preach the gospel. Defying the court, Hovey insisted he would continue to preach until the authorities 'cut out his tongue.' The case was taken to Halifax, where the Council dismissed the charges and found the Quarter Sessions action 'irregular.'[12] Although Alline does not mention this influence in his autobiography – he was perhaps purposely vague about all such matters – the religious enthusiasm of the Minas Separates must have drawn him to them. From men like Dimock and Hovey, Alline undoubtedly acquired or strengthened a good many of his later positions. The Separates were clearly anti-authoritarian in their attitudes and actions. Convinced of the righteousness of their own doctrinal position and of the primacy of eternal salvation over earthly success, they did not hesitate to defy duly constituted authority in church and state. They rejected traditional Puritanism less for doctrinal reasons than over questions of emphasis and church practice.

Like the Separates, Henry Alline emphasized the need for the new birth and personal salvation over the maintenance of order in either church or state. Similarly, he was always extremely suspicious of formal institutions and rigid church practices, preferring instead to stress experience rather than organization. One of the strongest influences of the Separates upon Alline was undoubtedly their attitude towards the question of church membership. The Separates always insisted that the only criterion for membership, and admission to the sacraments, was the achievement of the new birth. Many of the more radical converts of the Great Awakening came to reject infant baptism as unscriptural, but the Separates always maintained that an individual's beliefs regarding baptism should not be a bar to communion with other saints. This position on 'open communion' soon broke down in New England, but the advocacy of Henry Alline perpetuated it in Nova Scotia.

The later insistence of Alline upon open communion between Baptists and non-Baptists ran counter to the tide not only in New England but in Nova Scotia as well. Even before Alline's emergence as an evangelical preacher in 1776, the strength of those who insisted on closed communion – particularly those who restricted the sacrament to individuals who had rejected infant baptism – was growing. The Annapolis valley was visited by several Baptist preachers in the 1760s, particularly John Sutton of Hopewell, New Jersey, who ministered to a congregation at Newport from 1766 to 1769, and Ebenezer Moulton, a Massachusetts Baptist preacher who emigrated to Yarmouth on the west coast of Nova Scotia in 1761. Moulton organized a Baptist church in Horton (Wolfville) in the mid 1760s, but he did not remain long in the community. Both Sutton and Moulton were 'New-Lights,' i.e., evangelical pietists, and Henry Alline undoubtedly was familiar with them. But however much the Baptists may have reinforced his pietism, their insistence on rigid standards of church membership apart from the new birth always repelled him. Nevertheless, others were won over, including several sons of Shubael Dimock and perhaps the older man as well.

Although Alline's acquaintanceship with Separates and Baptists in the formative years of his religious development is reasonably certain despite his own reticence about recording it, his familiarity with the Quaker and Anglican elements in his community is somewhat more problematic. Nevertheless, a small Quaker enclave did exist in Falmouth, and an Anglican missionary did regularly visit the township. It is possible that Alline and the Anglican Joseph Bennett did come into contact, and it may have been from Bennett that Alline obtained some of the Anglican devotional literature with which he was later familiar, particularly the writings of William Law. As for the Quakers, they and Alline certainly should have felt sympathetic vibrations. The Friends believed in the inner light, were anti-sacramental, anti-authoritarian, and anti-Calvinistic – all Alline's principles as well – and their rejection of the affairs of the world (including military service) was in full accord with Alline's fundamental teachings. Such similarities may not reflect any direct connection between the Quakers and Alline so much as they underline the parallels between the growth of the Society of Friends and the 'New-Light' movement which Alline came later to lead in Nova Scotia during the American Revolution. As a religious sect, the Quakers were principally a response to the tension, uncertainty, and violence of the English Civil War; many Englishmen responded to wartime conditions by searching for some permanence and assurance in religion. They found it with the Quakers, who emphasized a personal rather than a social religious experience, and rejected most of those standards of society which were associated with the war. In a similar way, Henry Alline's New-Light movement was a response to the uncertainty and tension of the era of the American Revolution, and many Nova Scotians, particularly those from New England, sought and found assurance in the new birth preached by Alline.

Whatever the impact of Separates, Baptists, Quakers, and Anglicans upon Alline, in the last analysis his environment and external circumstances beyond his control were the critical factors. He had reached assurance of conversion on 26 March 1775. Little more than three weeks later, the battles of Lexington and Concord signalled the opening of the war of the American Revolution. Nova Scotians had been aware of the growing chasm between Britain and her North American colonies. Most settlers had friends or relatives in New England or elsewhere who were rabid patriots prepared to fight for their beliefs. Nova Scotia, however, was far too dependent upon British assistance and far too disorganized socially and politically beyond Halifax to respond to grievances in an aggressive manner. So long as the disagreement remained verbal, Nova Scotians could vicariously support the Americans without damaging either themselves or their psyches. The opening of actual hostilities in Boston – where were stationed General Thomas Gage's regiments formerly based in Halifax – made it necessary for most residents of Nova Scotia to take some sort of stand, at least mentally. The vast majority chose not to support the rebels, a decision best suited to their own self-interest but one which cost something in self-respect. This decision was not made by the average settler instantaneously in April of 1775, but was reached over the succeeding year and a half of uncertainty,

personal, like Alline

virtually the same time-span during which Henry Alline was engaged in resolving his own knotty problem of whether or not he should respond to God's call to preach.

For a variety of reasons, the problem of his call became inextricably interwoven for Alline with the dilemma of contending political loyalties. Along with many of his neighbours, Alline rejected New England and its rebellion. But he adopted a stance not simply of political neutralism but of withdrawal from politics combined with a renunciation of spiritual-religious-intellectual allegiances and ties as well. By withdrawing from the secular world of Nova Scotia, he indicated his dissatisfaction with the prevailing British establishment there. By rejecting Puritanism, he demonstrated that he was no slavish follower of the New England 'line' of rebellion and revolution which Puritanism had aided and abetted. Alline successfully disassociated himself from both sides in the revolutionary crisis, and his account of his debate over accepting a call to preach is revealing and symptomatic, perhaps even intentionally symbolic, of the response of many Nova Scotians to the dilemma posed by the American rebellion.

On 23 March 1775 Alline's immediate response to his call to preach was 'amen, Lord, I'll go, I'll go, send me, send me.' He realized what an unlikely preacher he would make, admitting:

my capacity in the world was low, being obliged to labour daily with my hands to get a living; my father's estate was not very large, and my parents being almost past labour, I had the whole care of these temporal concerns. As for learning, it was true I had read and studied more than was common for one in my station, but my education was but small: what I had of human literature, I had acquired of myself without schooling, excepting what I had obtained before I was eleven years of age, for I never went to school, after I came to Nova Scotia.[13]

Among other things, this statement certainly underlines Alline's credentials as a Nova Scotian, and a not untypical one at that.

After the initial enthusiasm of his conversion had worn off, however, the obstacle of education became a serious problem. This feeling of an impediment unquestionably had its roots in New England. Puritanism in New England had always insisted on a learned ministry, one conversant with the 'tongues' (Latin, Greek, and Hebrew), an attainment achieved only through university education which was a New England monopoly. Henry could not easily reject this standard, noting:

the prejudices of education and the strong ties of tradition so chained me down, that I could not think of myself qualified for it, without having a great deal of human learning; and although I sometimes had not the least doubt, but God had called me to the ministry, yet I could not believe, that it was his will, that I should preach, until he had found some way to get me qualified by human assistance.[14]

In April or May of 1775, Alline had discussed the problem with one of his brothers-in-law, probably John Payzant, who also 'was under the chains ... respecting human learning.' He advised Alline to read and study, until 'some door opened ... to attain to more learning.'

His future remained uncertain until October of 1775, although Alline was still drawn to New England. He finally decided that he 'could not preach' until he 'had acquired learning, and therefore must proceed to New-England, and endeavour some way or other to get learning there.' He had little money, but with his parents' consent he set out for Boston, where he had 'many relations.'[15] At this time the military and political implications of the American rebellion were still not entirely clear to most Nova Scotians. Town meetings held in the summer of 1775 supported New England, though many residents signed declarations of loyalty to the Crown. A good deal of movement of people between Nova Scotia and New England still was possible, particularly on vessels supplying General Gage's occupation army in Boston with Nova Scotia foodstuffs. New England privateers were active in preying on this trade. The Nova Scotia government had only begun to raise a military force to defend the province, and New Englanders in the province were only starting to fear 'the danger of young men being pressed to go to war.' In Cornwallis, the port from which Henry was to board a vessel for Boston, he discovered that the vessel 'was seized, and would not get clear until the Spring.' Hearing that his family had caught the small pox and desired him to return to them, he gave up all thoughts of New England and returned to Falmouth, where inoculations against the dread disease saved and protected almost everyone.[16]

In November of 1775 the government in the province decided to call up one-fifth of the provincial militia under the command of Henry Denny Denson. This action forced the inhabitants to a conscious decision on their position relative to the war. Many refused to serve, and the government had difficulty finding officers. Henry Alline was 'solicited by some of the officers to put in for a commission in the militia.' He refused, though he had some regrets until the Lord showed him 'the vanity of all things here below and the worth of souls.' He saw that his only commission should be one 'from heaven to go forth, and enlist my fellow-mortals to fight under the banners of Jesus Christ.'[17] Alline had faced up to the British establishment and had positively rejected it, finding a religious justification for pursuing a policy outlined by the inhabitants of Yarmouth in a petition to the government:

We were almost all of us born in New England, we have Fathers, Brothers & Sisters in that country, divided betwixt natural affection to our nearest relations, and good Faith and Friendship to our King and Country, we want to ... be permitted at this time to live in a peaceable State, as we look on to be the only situation in which we with our Wives and Children, can be in any tolerable degree safe.[18]

Like the Acadians before them, the New Englanders in the face of external crisis desired 'to be neuter.'

Although the militia callup forced many Nova Scotians to seek refuge in neutrality, they – like Henry Alline – had still explicitly rejected only the British demand for their loyalties. In early 1776, however, rumours of an American invasion of Nova Scotia were being circulated in the province. By mid-April of that year Henry Alline 'began to see that I had all this time been led astray by labouring so much after human learning and wisdom, and had held back from the call of God.' On 18 April, a day 'set apart for fasting and prayer' on the eve of the first anniversary of Lexington and Concord, Henry Alline 'came out and spoke by way of exhortation,' but he was still a little uncertain. The chronology as recorded in his autobiography is a bit unclear, but it was apparently on 19 April 1776 that Alline made his final decision to begin a public preaching career.[19] He would have been hard put to find a more symbolic date for making a final break with the New England traditions which had hitherto held him back. On 19 April he became an emancipated man, free of British institutions and Yankee traditions. Henceforth Henry Alline was the 'New-Light preacher,' and he would offer to other Nova Scotians what he himself had found: a spiritual assurance which rejected and transcended the tribulations of the secular world, whether British or American. It was a message both conditioned by and suited to the age, and was unmistakably Nova Scotian in its emphasis.

3

The People Being Much Engaged and Awakened

In April of 1776 Henry Alline began an itinerant preaching career which ended only with his death on 2 February 1784 in New Hampshire. At the time of his decision to answer the call to preach, Alline was 28 years old. Neatly but plainly dressed, he did not present a prepossessing public figure, being of 'medium size, straight, thin of body, light complexion, light curly hair, and dreamy blue eyes.'[1] However ordinary in physical appearance, Alline had nevertheless certain intangible qualities of charisma and leadership which made him long remembered by Nova Scotians. Even before his conversion, he had by his own admission been the principal leader of the young people in his community, and he was considered of sufficient standing to be offered a militia commission by the government in 1776. Whether at the beginning of his preaching career there were any indications of the tubercular condition which ultimately cut short his life is uncertain, but in later years he showed signs of what contemporaries called consumption – a sickly, pale physical appearance contrasting with a hyperactive, occasionally feverish, mental state.

The Nova Scotia within which Alline began his preaching career was a tension-racked province. Although a 'rebel' invasion did not occur until October of 1776, when Colonel Jonathan Eddy of Cumberland led an abortive attack on Fort Cumberland not too far from the Annapolis valley, rumours of an invasion had been floating about the province for nearly a year. Eddy's forces were recruited mainly from Machias, Passamaquoddy, and Maugerville (the latter two communities in what was to become New Brunswick), and he was joined by only a few New Englanders from the Minas townships. The 'invasion' was easily driven off in November of 1776, and warfare in Nova Scotia thereafter 'settled down to its exhausting, nerve racking forms – privateering, counter-privateering, the establishment and destruction of privateer bases, and the uncertain business of rival bidding for the friendship of the Indians near the Maine boundary.'[2]

From the time of his decision to preach in April of 1776 to his formal ordination as an 'Itinerant Preacher' three years later, Alline confined his activities to the region around the Minas basin. Uncertainties of travel in these years when privateering was rampant in the waters off Nova Scotia tended to keep him close to home, as did his own lack of confidence in his reception in strange communities. But it was probably Alline's relationship with his family which was the basic factor in limiting his evangelical circuit. He may have succeeded in breaking free of primary political and cultural allegiances to Britain and New England, but he had not yet succeeded in emancipating himself from family loyalties. The acceptance of the preaching call got him out of the house but not out of the family circle. Not surprisingly, his parents initially opposed his preaching, 'as sometimes to leave the house as I was speaking.'³ To some extent they may have retained a commitment to Puritan traditions with which Alline had broken, but they undoubtedly also recognized in Henry's new vocation a threat to his continued presence as effectual head of the household. In the long run, however, Alline's parents could not deny Christ any more than he could.

By 1779 military threats were lessened, Henry had built up confidence in his abilities, and his parents had been won over. The result was his ordination as an evangelist on 6 April of that year by three Annapolis Valley churches. The most important part of the ceremony was the handing over to Alline of 'my credentials signed by the delegates.'⁴ These provided a formal basis for the extension of his itinerant activities into the remainder of Maritime Canada and ultimately into the United States. In 1779 he entered the Cumberland region of Nova Scotia (much of which became part of New Brunswick) and the Saint John River valley, particularly Maugerville, a community depressed in mind and spirit after the Eddy fiasco of 1776. His ever widening circuit in 1781 grew to include the New England fishing communities on the southern and western shores of Nova Scotia. In 1782 he undertook a journey to the Island of St. John (now Prince Edward Island) and in 1783 he set forth for New England.

Although his evangelical techniques undoubtedly improved with experience, Henry Alline maintained much the same method of operation throughout his entire career. Like most successful evangelists, he had his own distinctive style, but his general approach was based upon well-known and long-tested principles of revivalism refined during the Great Awakening: itinerant preaching in any available place; extemporaneous sermons designed for dramatic conversions; lay participation in religious services; emotional extravagance; and open confrontation with those who opposed evangelical principles.

From the beginning of his ministry, Alline travelled continually and seldom spent more than a few days in any one township or locality. Even when his circuit had become greatly widened to include areas which required lengthy and difficult journeys to reach, he remained in one place only briefly and away from his central base in the Minas townships for no more than a few months; he never did completely free himself from his family. Most of his early travelling in the basin was done on horseback, and he not uncommonly rode forty to fifty miles in a single day. He usually journeyed to places more distant from his home (such as the Saint John valley or the south shore townships) by boat, and indeed moved from community to community by whatever form of transportation was available. On one occasion, he and a young man who carried his saddlebags hiked forty miles in five days on snowshoes; on another, he walked over twenty miles overland before horses were obtained to continue the journey. Neither bad weather nor his own disabilities ever delayed Alline. He hiked on one cold January day when, he wrote, 'I often had scales of ice on my face and eyes, for the snow blowed very thick all the day,' but after resting the night in a tiny house he was able to resume the journey the following morning.[5] Frequently accompanied on his sojourns by those who had become converted or were simply curious, he employed the time to preach to and exhort his companions.

In the many communities where facilities for public meetings were lacking and in others where the meeting-house was closed to him by the incumbent minister, Alline preached of necessity in private houses, in barns, or in the open air. Outdoor services were quite commonly held, partly because more could thus be accommodated, partly because they enabled Alline to preach by the water's edge as he travelled by boat or by the roadside as he made his way from one village to another. He did not consider either a formal church edifice or money of much priority in his scale of spiritual values. Like all good evangelists, he brought religion to the people, and his willingness to journey and preach under all conditions struck a responsive chord among Nova Scotians still struggling (particularly outside the more settled communities) on the brink of survival. Settlers lacking the means to support clergymen of the more orthodox churches could scarcely avoid contrasting Alline and his fellow evangelists with other clergymen of 'worldly' values who were concerned with matters such as regular salaries and their own physical comfort. In many scattered and isolated areas Alline was the first clergyman ever seen, and fully aware of the hardships he had experienced to reach them, the people were favourably disposed to him before he actually began his preaching.

Unlike the settled clergyman – particularly the Puritan one – who laboriously prepared his weekly or bi-weekly sermon and read it from the pulpit, the evangelist relied on extemporaneous preaching. Alline was no exception here, and he frequently preached three or four times a day in different locations. Because the usual sermon was improvised, it is difficult to tell whether the samples of Alline's sermons which reached the public press are entirely typical of his technique. But as the published sermons and several diary entries indicate, Alline apparently followed the usual evangelical practice of beginning with a biblical text into which was woven the central message of revival. He had a standard series of points which he desired to make and a firm grasp of the biblical idiom in which to couch them. Constant movement made it unnecessary to maintain a large stock of different sermons since no one in his audience would hear more than a few at any time. Alline was capable of developing on the spot a sermon on any biblical text. On one occasion, an 'enemy to the cause' challenged him 'to preach from a particular text he would give me.' As Alline recorded,

I told him I would not preach to satisfy curiosity, because I must labour for the good of society; but would as willingly preach from one text as from another, if the Lord gave it to me. He said, he desired no more, and then mentioned the text, which seemed immediately to be given to me, and took hold of my mind. I told him I would preach from it for it was a blessed text. I then went in and preached, and it was the most powerful meeting I ever saw in that country.[6]

Response to such a challenge was a part of Alline's method.

The main message of any of Alline's sermons was the need for immediate recognition of the danger to one's soul and the need for the 'new birth,' a conversion experience which would parallel his own. Most of his audience apparently understood this message, although frequently in a rather simplistic form. One listener explained that 'Henry Alline was a "New Light" and that the "New Light" were the people of God for they were Christians and that none could go to Heaven unless they were converted.'[7] The evangelist's task was not solely one of preaching the gospel, however. As Alline recorded on one of many similar occasions, 'the people being much engaged and awakened, were with me continually, so that I was preaching, praying, exhorting or discoursing, almost all the time, from early in the morning, till twelve at night.'[8] Although he revelled in such activity, particularly when it seemed to be producing results, it was still exhausting and probably helped contribute to his early death.

All good evangelists have of necessity to be students of mass behaviour, with a fine sense of how to employ crowd reaction for their purposes. Although his own conversion had been an intensely private experience, Alline soon realized that a spiritual awakening was easier to induce in public gatherings. He encouraged participation by his audience in the worship service and employed a large number of hymns (many of which he himself had written in the absence of hymnals) in the hours of praying and singing which comprised one of his gatherings. Alline's hymns were clearly in the English tradition led by Isaac Watts and Charles Wesley, and they are deserving of much more attention than they have hitherto received from students both of hymnology and of Canadian literature.[9] Much of what Alline produced was little more than awkward versifying, but at his best – and particularly when he was not working in strict verse patterns of metre and rhyme – he was capable of exciting work. Love was one of his favourite themes:

> Ah like itself breaks forth unbounded Love
> To fill the void of ev'ry hungry Mind
> That pants to drink from that o'er flowing Sea;
> Nor can that ancient Fountain be contain'd.
> O Love Divine transform me like Thyself
> That when the fleeting Scenes of Mortal Climes
> (And Sin, thou Foe!) all in Oblivion sunk
> To gaze on thee all ravish'd with the View
> (Ah humble Seat) I'll found while Thought is known
> Thy worthy Fame in one begining Song
>   (My God!) that grand immortal Note! AMEN[10]

One of his most popular hymns – so well regarded that contemporaries preserved it in manuscript – concluded:

Wounded Hearts may now Rejoice
Mourners hear the Saviours Voice
Hasten to the Courts Above
There to Sing Redeeming Love

Soon from all the Storms of Night
We to Heaven will take our Flight
Winged on the Celestial Dove
Sailing in Redeeming Love

Love shall be our Lasting Theme
Love shall Every Soul Inflame
Always Now in Realms Above
Ah, Amen Redeeming Love[.][11]

Alline's verse is discussed briefly in most text books in Canadian literature, but a full-scale analysis of it has never been undertaken, and is much needed.

In addition to singing, those who had experienced grace were encouraged to speak out and tell their experiences. At Windsor, one woman 'who had come fourteen miles to hear the gospel' was

delivered from the bondage of sin, and the borders of eternal perdition, and brought to the glorious liberty of the children of God. She was so overjoyed, that she could not contain, but cried out in divine raptures, with shouts of praise to God, and exhorting souls to come and share with her.[12]

Several of Alline's followers, including his brother-in-law John Payzant and Thomas Handley Chipman, began their own ministerial careers by 'exhorting' at public meetings.

Opponents of Alline and other evangelists in Nova Scotia and elsewhere criticized them for encouraging 'emotional extravagances.' From Alline's point of view, most of the population were unconverted sinners sunk in 'darkness,' and any means which helped to encourage the true spirit of redeeming Christ was hardly to be condemned. In Liverpool, Alline recorded with obvious and genuine pleasure that

many were brought out of darkness and rejoiced, and exhorted in public. And O how affecting it was to see some young people not only exhort their companions, but also take their parents by the hand, and entreat them for their soul's sake to rest no longer in their sins, but fly to Jesus Christ while there was hope. One young lad (who turned out to be a very bright christian) I saw, after sermon, take his father by the hand, and cry out, O father, you have been a great sinner, and now are an old man: an old sinner, with grey hairs upon your head, going right down to destruction. O turn, turn, dear father, return and fly to Jesus Christ: with many other such like expressions and entreaties, enough to melt a stony heart.

One critic in the crowd yelled out, 'that is damned foolishness.' Alline's response was simple and crushing: 'I looked upon him, and charged him to cease, and likewise to remember what his doom would be, that dares to blaspheme to the gospel of the Lord Jesus Christ.'[13] Not only was Alline able to deal effectively with critics and 'opposers,' as he called them, but he clearly enjoyed doing so. It was an essential part of the constant combat against godlessness and darkness, of course, but such encounters also usually worked out to his advantage.

Most of Alline's opposers, especially in the early years of his ministry, were clerical leaders of the organized churches, especially the Presbyterians. In the disturbed war years, the New England ministers were, on the whole, too few and weak to attack Alline, and it was not until 1781, when he and Jonathan Scott of Yarmouth had a confrontation, that Alline came face-to-face with a New England opponent as determined as he was. Scott was a contemporary of Alline, having been born in Lunenberg, Massachusetts, in 1744 and having come to Nova Scotia in 1764. Like Alline, Scott spent the hard years of the 1760s as a farmer, but unlike the evangelist, he married and started to raise a family. In 1770 Scott began preaching in the church at Jebogue (Yarmouth), and in 1772 – though lacking university education – he went to New England to become formally ordained as minister over the Yarmouth church. Scott would later receive a dismissal from his people and move (in 1792) to what is today Maine, but in 1781 he was in control of his congregation and saw himself as the principal Puritan opponent of Alline's evangelicalism.[14]

Both Scott and Alline recorded their versions of the 1781 meetings. The two accounts are not incompatible, but indicate clearly that each man sought to couch his in terms most favourable to himself. According to the evangelist, he and Scott met at the home of a local deacon, and Scott 'raged so to my face that I was obliged to tell him, that allowing I was ever so wrong, for he had discovered a murdering spirit in that rage and wrangling, which I told him was far from the spirit and ways of Jesus; and at last his passion was so high, that he left the house.'[15] Scott admitted that on this occasion he told Alline 'that his *Impudence had fitted him for his Work.*' But in Scott's account this interchange had been preceded by a long discussion some days earlier in the more hospitable atmosphere of Scott's home. Here Scott had stated his reasons for opposing Alline, who replied, 'with an *Air* of *Contempt* and *Disdain,* "I have Nothing to say; you have settled the Point, and have termed me an Imposture, and have censured me very high." ' Nevertheless, not until after dinner did Alline leave Scott's home and not until later did he respond to Scott's accusations.[16]

Earlier, in 1776 at Cornwallis, 'the standing minister of, and then at the place, came to hear and seemed determined to dash me,' but Benajah Phelps, an 'uncompromising Whig' who had been dismissed by his congregation 'on account of some division,' was hardly in a strong position to exercise much influence.[17] The Scots Presbyterian clergy of the Cumberland region, virtual autocrats in their congregations and staunch royalists, were much stronger critics, although they met with little success. Alline experienced only token opposition from the Anglican missionaries, partly because there were so few of them in the back country where he travelled and partly because he was not particularly active among Anglican communicants. No direct controversy between Alline and his principal evangelical rivals, the Methodists, ever erupted, but he and William Black, the Methodist leader, certainly contended for public support, especially in the Cumberland area. The absence of conflict with the Methodists was probably largely a result of the high regard which Black always held for Alline. In 1783 Black wrote to Alline (who by this time was 'very ill in body') :

Although we differ in sentiment, let us manifest our love to each other. I always admired your gifts and graces, and affectionately loved your person, although I could never receive your peculiar opinions. But shall we on this account destroy the work of God? God forbid! May the Lord take away all bigotry, and fill us with pure, genuine, catholic love![18]

For his part, Alline was not so certain that Black had ever experienced a 'saving change of heart.'

Although Alline saw public disputations with the opposition as 'very unprofitable,' and hoped to guard 'against such waste of time, for I would rather have the enemy say, that I was afraid to hold the contest than to be guilty of spending time so unprofitably,' he was never able to keep this resolution. His own assurance of his duty and righteousness contributed to continued confrontations, but so too did an awareness that he generally came out ahead, at least in the minds of the public for which both sides contended. In Truro, deep in the heart of Presbyterian country, he faced on his first visit a public opinion which led the settlers to 'gaze at me, as I passed their doors, with as much strangeness, as if I was one of the antediluvians,' and he was even refused a room at the public house. A three-hour disputation – which the opposition ended in disgust – led the audience to declare 'that they were satisfied, and that they now saw and were astonished at what prejudice and false reports had done.' Thus, concluded Alline, 'the enemies of Christ, by their endeavouring to shut the door against the gospel, were the means of opening it.'[19]

Jonathan Scott subsequently accused Alline of publicly overstating the vehemence of the opposition he had met, which 'gained him Pity, to all Appearance, and served to enflame the People, and promote the End, no Doubt, which he aimed at.'[20] Certainly, even without misrepresentation, Alline's opposers did little more than win him sympathy and a sizeable audience for his activities which might otherwise not have gathered. Alline's defence of his mission was a good one; he had plenty of practice in developing arguments which were unassailable given his assumptions, and like most pietists he infuriated his opposition with an assurance which some called arrogance. In his early years, the bulk of the opposition concentrated their attack on Alline's right to preach. After 1781, when the evangelist began to publish books setting forth a rather unorthodox doctrinal position, he encountered more serious criticism. But much of his following did not care about doctrinal subtleties, and his books apparently did not circulate widely in the province before his death. A certain negative reaction to his doctrine in some of the New England townships, however, may help explain his decision to widen his ministry to more isolated areas.

The principal thrust of the opposition was easily handled by Alline. Most of his clerical critics asserted that he had no right to intrude on their territory, for they were the duly ordained ministers in the area and Alline nothing but a semi-literate lay exhorter without credentials, who was breaking up congregations and causing schism. Opponents never accepted Alline's ordination in 1779 as legitimate. This was a simple attack for Alline to demolish. He began with the assertion that all Christians should have experienced the new birth, for without it one was a creature of legalism, lacking saving grace. He moved from this point to brand his opponent as a 'Pharisee,' arguing:

all the high-priests, scribes and pharisees, who opposed the work of God, and crucified the Lord of Glory, had the same pretences, and made the same excuses, as you do; they would not acknowledge, that they were crucifying the Lord of Glory, or opposing the work of God, but said, they were only bearing a testimony against imposters, and deluded men, to obstruct errors; and enthusiasm creeping into the house of God, &c. you say, this is not right, and that is not right... And was this not the language of all the enemies of Christ before you even from the beginning of the world, and had they not the same reasons for opposing all the servants of God, when sent among them?[21]

Having shifted the burden of proof to his opponent, Alline was in position to follow up his own advantage. Should the critic insist that his own spiritual credentials were impeccable, Alline could then query why he was not out attacking those 'meeting for carnal mirth, spending hours over a bottle of wine in all manner of vain discourse, and the young people frolicking and playing at cards,' instead of bothering those 'meeting often for the worship of God' where 'those young people, instead of frolicking and singing carnal songs are praying and singing psalms, hymns and spiritual songs, exhorting their companions to fly from the wrath to come.' It was a difficult argument to counter.

For those who insisted on pressing further to question Alline's educational background and his right to preach, the answers were reasonably simple. Alline did not 'reject natural abilities, nor human learning when brought in their proper place ... , but their being brought in, to supply the want of divine assistance and authority from heaven, has already been the means of large spreading and supporting the cause of anti-christ.' An educated man might understand the letter of the gospel, but what mattered was its spirit. Alline did not despise learning, but 'I must acknowledge it appears to me very needless to be at too much pains in pursuit' of education, 'only to attain the name of a collegian.' The Lord, after all, does not say that 'colleges, universities, bishops, priests, or presbyteries are the way or the door; but he saith I am the way and I am the door.' The ordination and licensing of ministers were nothing more than steps by the enemies of Christ to produce 'a snare for immortal souls.' For those who traced ordination back to the church at Rome, Alline queried: are then the Roman Catholic priests true ministers of the gospel? The standard Protestant answer was 'Of course not, for they are not true Christians.' Then whatever makes a true Christian makes a true minister of the gospel, and the essential qualification is that a man be regenerate, 'a man with a new born soul, a man that hath been restored to God from his fallen state, that hath been slain by the law and made alive by the gospel, and thereby he knoweth the terrors of the law, the power and sweetness of the everlasting gospel.' Not all true Christians could be ministers, for many lacked the proper gifts and abilities, but they should not be prevented from preaching. Hopefully, they would themselves discover 'the place and station, for which God hath designed them.'[22]

For Henry Alline, the essence of Christianity was the new birth, and all other aspects of religion, which in general detracted from concentration on the essentials, were nothing but the devil's work, traps of the anti-Christ. He denied that he favoured schisms or separations in a church of Christ, but of course most so-called churches were not in his view churches of Christ. Echoing the sentiments of centuries of reformers, Alline argued that to remain in a church sunk 'in the form of godliness without the power' was 'not holding up the powers of darkness to their destruction,' but, more important, it was 'taking an effectual step to bring death and darkness' upon one's precious soul.[23]

Although in his writings Alline devoted a good deal of attention to his opposition, its force and importance should not be overemphasized. On the whole, most Nova Scotians with whom he came into contact were not only sympathetic to his mission, but psychologically and emotionally ready for his message. Alline intuitively concentrated his activities in those areas most likely to be receptive to him, although not all shared exactly the same reason or combination of reasons for being so responsive. He did not visit Halifax until 1781, and then only to get a book 'from the press'; he found the city a 'land of darkness' offering him no opportunity to preach the gospel.[24] In general, Alline concentrated his efforts on rural and frontier Nova Scotia. Here much of the population was living close to the edge of economic disaster and in a state of discontented rootlessness. Moreover, the rural and back-country people were predisposed to favour revival and were frequently living without churches and clergymen. All of these problems were exacerbated by the American Revolution.[25]

The religious awakening Alline touched off was hardly a safety-valve which drew the attention of New England residents of Nova Scotia from revolution to revival. The province was not in a state of evangelical fervour in 1776, and religious enthusiasm seemed to build only as the military and political threat declined. Nevertheless, the Great Awakening and the American Revolution were clearly closely related phenomena in Nova Scotia. The revival does not explain the political situation, but the agitation, unrest, and dislocation produced by the Revolution certainly contributed to the reaction of many in the province (especially New Englanders) to the evangelical message preached by Henry Alline and those who followed in his footsteps. At the same time, care must be taken not to attribute too much to the political crisis. The Maritimes were ripe for revival even before Lexington and Concord. The Revolution helped provide an instrument of Awakening in the person of Alline, and heightened the sense of dissatisfaction and discontent in many rural parts of the province.

As a newly settled area, the Maritimes naturally experienced economic difficulties, some regions less than others. The Annapolis valley, with the best agricultural lands in the province, was far more prosperous than the Chignecto peninsula, the coastal fishing ports, the Island of St. John, or the mainland settlements in Sunbury County. A new arrival to the Island of St. John in 1775, for example, wrote

When we arrived at new London I was mutch Surprized to see what a place it was, It being so very different from the Idea I had formed of it. I then begin to repent of my Voyage and wish my Selfe in Old London again; but wishes and repentance was now too late; but I soon came to the determination of leaving this place as soon as possible from the first View. At first Entering New London from the Woods it was cut down within a quarter of a mile of the first house when from the path on our right we could see a little row of Log houses and one large house on our left in all about Sixteen houses... I soon found my friend Compton & Wife ... were badly off for provisions having nothing but Salt Codfish and Potatoes with plenty of good Water.[26]

Although the Annapolis valley may have been able to sell its agricultural surplus to the troops during the war, communities like New London, and there were many of them in the Maritimes, obviously had no surplus to sell. For Halifax and a few of the wealthier traders in the outports, there may have been profits from wartime trading, but for the average settler on the seacoast the Revolution meant privateer raids and the danger of capture or disaster at sea as well as the interrupted shipment of much needed supplies from outside.

If not all communities felt equally the discontent born of immediate economic hardship, all shared in the psychological uneasiness born of having pulled up roots elsewhere to settle in Nova Scotia. The emotional individualism characteristic of evangelical pietism has always flourished under the unstable conditions of fragmentation and mobility which accompany any major migration of people, whether from one continent to another or from countryside to city. Since such movement frequently means at least short-term economic hardship, as it certainly did in Nova Scotia, it is difficult to make a clear separation between the two factors. But even areas which enjoyed relative prosperity still experienced the dissatisfaction familiar to anyone who has cut himself off from relatives and friends and has not created new relationships with neighbours. By the very nature of its recent settlement, Nova Scotia was populated by rootless people. In many rural areas, particularly the prosperous ones, the movement of the population to individual farmsteads sealed the failure of village communities which might have compensated for broken ties of family and friendship. The coming of the American Revolution was the final straw, especially for New Englanders, since if they remained in Nova Scotia they were forced to a conscious break with their former friends and relations. The last tenuous emotional tie with 'home' was cut, and the other-worldly ethic of pietism provided both an outlet and a rationale for the crisis of identity faced by many in the province.

Economic hardship and rootlessness, therefore, made almost all rural Nova Scotians susceptible in various degrees to revivalism. Particularly receptive were the New Englanders, who also had strong religious reasons for being favourably disposed to the phenomenon. Almost everyone brought up in New England had learned from childhood of the importance of an experience of conversion – as had Henry Alline himself – and many older folk had been exposed to the Great Awakening which had occurred in that region in the 1740s. Nova Scotia 'Yankees' viewed wistfully those halcyon days when spiritual concern had swept the countryside and when religion mattered. Moreover, the coming of the Revolution greatly weakened the tenuous grip which organized religion (particularly American Puritanism) had on much of the province. The Puritan churches of Nova Scotia – always in trouble – had lost all but four of their ministers by 1777, and several of these were under suspicion of sympathizing with the rebels. The only two clergymen unaffected by the political situation were Israel Cheever of Liverpool and Jonathan Scott of Jebogue (Yarmouth), both serving fishing ports on the southwestern shores of the province. Anglican missionaries withdrew from service in most areas of Nova Scotia at the outbreak of hostilities, and the New England townships of the Minas basin, the Chignecto peninsula, and the Saint John River valley were virtually bereft of spiritual leadership except for the few Presbyterian ministers in the Scottish settlements in Cumberland County, who never really attempted to fill the void. The itinerant evangelical activities of Henry Alline and his disciples were ideally designed to fill this spiritual vacuum.

Although Alline's revival was not directly responsible for the failure of Nova Scotians to support the rebels – there were more immediate reasons for not doing so – the political crisis added additional tension to a province already predisposed to revivalism. Perhaps inadvertently, the Awakening in Nova Scotia became something of a counter-revolutionary force. Henry Alline had no interest in secular politics, and would have denied as vehemently that he was a reactionary as that he was a radical. But through the confluence of circumstances beyond his control and even beyond his comprehension, Alline was both. Fortunately for the British government, Alline's radicalism was directed almost exclusively against New England Puritanism and its traditions. But since these represented a critical component of New England's tenuous ties with many Nova Scotians, every blow which Alline struck against Puritan authority helped widen the already considerable gap between the rebellious colonies and the province. The British establishment came ultimately to view the evangelical pietism of revivalism as dangerous subversive influence in Maritime Canada and elsewhere in British North America – and in many ways it was – but one result of Alline's career was to destroy completely American Puritanism in Canada, for which the authorities should have been grateful. Nevertheless, to see the Great Awakening in Nova Scotia only in a political context would be a great mistake.

Whatever the motivations of Alline and his followers, whatever the results of their actions, the Great Awakening in Nova Scotia was principally a movement of spiritual reform much like those which had over the centuries convulsed Christianity. The historical movements which most closely paralleled and preconditioned the pietistic Awakening in Nova Scotia were the Puritan reform impulse in 16th- and 17th-century England, and the Great Awakening in 18th-century New England. All these movements had in common a re-emphasis on regenerate man and the rejection of the formalism of the existing churches; all emphasized the individual voluntarism of the sect over the social comprehension of the church. Had Alline so chosen, he could have stressed his agreement with many of the great Puritan reformers, especially in terms of organization and polity. His position on structure was one which had much in common with earlier Puritanism in its heyday of reform, and Alline can quite legitimately be viewed as an unconscious heir of great Puritan Separatists such as John Robinson or Robert Browne. In terms of polity, Alline probably rejected the Puritan reform tradition less than did the Methodists, his principal competitors, whose form of ecclesiastical organization was highly structured and hierarchical.

Alline, then, was not really assailing historical Puritanism (which he probably never understood and whose divines he had not read) but only its Nova Scotian manifestations – or perversions. Unfortunately, he was never able to stabilize in Nova Scotia all of the principles of church organization to which he was most committed, and the

result was that he destroyed rather than created. But this was not because he lacked a positive program. To a limited extent, the Baptists
in Nova Scotia inherited Alline's general position, but they were far
less militant and individualistic than Alline on most points except for
the rejection of infant baptism, a matter which Alline preferred not to
emphasize.

Although Henry Alline never produced a single and unified statement of his program for ecclesiastical organization, its main outlines
are clear from scattered references in his writings and from his activities in organizing churches in Nova Scotia from 1776 to 1782. These
churches constituted his institutional legacy to religious life in Nova
Scotia. The first church which he gathered was, naturally enough, at
Falmouth and Newport in September 1776. In July of 1778 a church
in Cornwallis and Horton (Wolfville) was founded with Alline's assistance, and he co-operated in the organization of a Baptist church
in Horton on October of the same year. It was these three churches
that had collaborated in April of 1779 to ordain Alline as an 'Itinerant Preacher.' Alline's first tour into the area north of the Bay of
Fundy resulted in the reorganization of the Maugerfield (or Maugerville) church in 1779 in accordance with his 'New-Light' principles.
In 1780 a church composed of inhabitants from the Annapolis County
townships of Granville, Annapolis, and Wilmot was created, and late
in 1782 one was founded in the south shore community of Liverpool.
Most of these churches continued to rely on Alline as pastor until his
death. In his absence worship services were carried on by the deacons.
This was a time-honoured arrangement in the North American back
country, and one which was continued by the Maritime Baptists. If
the church and its members prospered, a resident minister might
ultimately be sought, but in the meantime an evangelist served as
preacher.

As was typical of the founding of 'come-outer' churches in 18th-century America, none of those associated with Henry Alline was organized in communities which considered themselves satisfied with the services of less pietistic and more settled pastors. In Yarmouth, where Jonathan Scott was active, energetic, and well liked, pietism made some inroads but did not produce a formal organization. Newport-Falmouth, Horton, and Maugerville all were totally destitute of clerical leadership, and earlier church organizations had disintegrated. In these communities, a New-Light church was filling a religious and spiritual void. At Cornwallis, Annapolis, and Liverpool, Puritan Congregational ministers were all engaged in acrimonious disputations with their parishioners over salaries long before the introduction of evangelical enthusiasm had occurred, and pietism gained from the conflict. The New-Lights did not so much overturn the settled churches as take advantage of their difficulties. The organizational principles enunciated by Henry Alline and other New-Lights were perfectly designed to exploit weaknesses. The New-Light program was not, however, one which could easily adjust to less chaotic and more stable conditions. Methodism's hierarchical and more formalized institutional structure was much better able to consolidate the gains of evangelicalism and to survive temporary lulls in popular enthusiasm. The New-Light churches were formed in periods of chaos and crisis, and had certain built-in tendencies toward instability which ultimately destroyed – or at least profoundly altered – them.

A large measure of responsibility for the institutional difficulties of the Nova Scotia New-Light movement rests ultimately with its founder. Part of the explanation is that he was too much the evangelical, not sufficiently concerned with matters of routine organization and structure. His basic interest was in conversion, not in the sacraments or the form of ecclesiastical polity. Had he lived longer, he might well have seen the need for new emphases; Alline's career coincided almost exactly with the years of revolutionary upheaval in North America, and he never faced a period of stability. Moreover, what organizational principles Alline did emphasize tended to be difficult to maintain over the long haul. This was particularly true of his position on infant baptism. Again, had he not died in 1784, he might have come to recognize this as a problem. As it was, in his brief career Henry Alline was always the religious prophet, never really the priest.

The basis of New-Light church organization was the commitment of the evangelical pietist that the only true Christians were those who had undergone the new birth, the crisis conversion. Since those who had not experienced saving grace were by definition outside Christianity, they obviously did not belong within a true church of Christ, which was 'a number of True Believers by an Acquaintence in the Fellowship of the Gospel, Voluntarily and understandingly Covenanting and embodying together for the maintaining of the Worship of God.' To ensure that only those who had enjoyed 'a Work of Grace in their Hart' were admitted to membership, candidates were required to relate publicly their experiences or to be tested by private delegates. Only those for whom existed 'Good Scriptural evidence and Soul Satisfying Knowledge' of 'union to Jesus Christ' were eligible to participate in the sacrament of the Lord's Supper.[27]

The other sacrament which the New Lights accepted was that of baptism. Here was a problem, since 'Real Believers' held 'different Sentiments ... Respecting that Ordinance,' some approving baptism of infants and others rejecting it, some preferring sprinkling and others immersion. With the exception of the Horton church, which always restricted membership to those who denied infant baptism, early New-Light churches in Nova Scotia opened communion to 'those that practice either by Sprinkling or Immersion either to Infants or Adults.' As had been the case thirty years earlier in New England, this policy resulted in a good many conflicts among the church membership, and Alline's diary mentions these continually from 1776 to his death. Alline always viewed the questions of mode and subjects of baptism as 'non-essential matters,' and constantly bemoaned 'that ever christians should contend about that, which never was nor never will be of any benefit to their souls ..., instead of contending for the truth as it is in Jesus.'[28] But even among his closest followers, Thomas Handley Chipman was an antipedobaptist, and by the beginning of the 19th century, only John Payzant held out among New-Light ministers for the Alline position. Once it was agreed that only true believers should belong to the Church of Christ, then logic demanded that infants (who have not experienced saving faith) be excluded from the sacraments of the church. Alline's view that the question was non-essential may have been reasonable, but, given the clashes within the churches over the issue, it was an impractical position, and only his great stature among the various flocks which considered him their pastor prevented disaster before his death.

Payzant and Chipman represented in their careers the two divergent wings of the New-Light movement in Nova Scotia. Both were ordained to open communion churches, Chipman at Annapolis in 1779 and Payzant at Cornwallis in 1786. Payzant left Cornwallis in the early 1790s following internal struggles over the question of baptism, and moved to Liverpool, where he succeeded Jonathan Scott and served as pastor from 1793 to his death in 1834. To the end of his life, John Payzant remained convinced that the question of the mode of baptism was one of little consequence to true Christians, and he was widely respected by Baptists like Chipman despite their disagreement with him. Chipman moved to the pastorate of the Nictaux Baptist Church in 1809, which he served until his death in 1830. In 1811 Chipman led his church to renounce open communion principles and become avowedly Baptist, a direction taken following bitter debates by most New-Lights in Nova Scotia.

Alline's prestige and relationship with the New-Light churches which he helped to organize obscured other organizational difficulties which later afflicted Nova Scotia New-Lights. The churches, for example, insisted on power to discipline those who behaved in an unchristian manner, and even maintained that 'Brethren in Christ ... aught not to go to Law one with another, but that all their differences aught to be decided by the Brethren.' This position ultimately resulted in a variety of disputes within churches over alleged wrongdoing, and in small communities, where everyone was acquainted with (or related to) everyone else, it produced continual quarrels as sides were chosen. Because of the insistence of the New-Light churches on congregational autonomy and internal democracy, no outside agency for adjudicating local disputes existed. The minister's position was limited, for he had 'no more Power in Church government than any other Brother excepting by the Superiority of [his] ... Gifts and Graces,' except that 'In case of A Tie' he was 'to have the Privilege of a Double Vote.' While Alline lived, he was able to exercise sufficient authority and moderation to keep conflict within manageable bounds. After his death, the disintegration of the churches which accompanied their shift to Baptist principles forced a later generation of Baptist ministers to organize a formal association to assist in keeping the peace.

In one final but extremely important matter, that of finances, Alline again avoided inherent difficulties by virtue of his own practice. Both because of the memory of disputes within the standing churches over finances and because of positive religious principle, the New-Lights opposed formal contracts with ministers and mandatory contribution for financial support. It was 'the Indispensible duty of all the Society as well as every member of the Church to Contribute toward the Support of the Gospel, and all other necessary charges that may arise in the Church according to their Several Abilities,' but this duty was voluntaristic, left to the believer's own conscience. Alline cared nothing for building formal structures in which to hold church meetings, and he was only interested in obtaining sufficient money to meet his very modest needs. At his death, his personal effects consisted of 'a horse and sleigh, his apparel, and about twelve dollars in money.'[29] As principal pastor for most of the New-Light churches during his lifetime, Alline provided spiritual service at minimal cost to the congregations. But this ideal situation could not continue long after his demise, and the New-Light churches had either to face up to increased expenditures or collapse.

In a very real sense, therefore, Henry Alline was not only the motivating but also the unifying element in the New-Light revival of Nova Scotia. Whether the movement, with all of its tenuous and unstable elements, could survive without his enthusiastic and altruistic leadership was something which no New-Light seriously considered. Alline is usually pictured as some sort of religious fanatic and zealot, but he was more than that. He was a brilliant leader whose principal failing was that his personal abilities obscured the inherent difficulties which his movement faced.

4

Some things in these Few Lines

Henry Alline has received little recognition as a literary and intellectual figure who must be taken seriously. For most of the chroniclers of evangelicalism in Nova Scotia, many of whom wrote in the 19th century, Alline was simply a pioneer itinerant evangelist. In this historical tradition, his literary activity was made to appear a peripheral and unimportant happenstance. To many commentators, Alline has thus appeared an anti-intellectual revivalist; to others, who recognized that he had attempted to grapple with what were for him the critical issues of his time, his thinking was confused and wrong-headed. But Henry Alline was more than a simple-minded evangelical; he was British Canada's most important and prolific intellectual voice in the 18th century, deserving far more recognition and attention than he has so far been accorded. It is perhaps another illustration of the prophet without honour in his own land that Alline's writings fell into almost immediate obscurity among his own countrymen and have been influential only in the United States, where they served as the ideological underpinnings of the Freewill Baptist movement founded by Benjamin Randall.

Alline's published writings were more numerous and substantial in content than those of any other Canadian of his time. He began writing for public consumption only after his ordination in 1779, and most of his works, although not all, were originally printed in Nova Scotia, the first appearing early in 1781. He wrote in odd moments snatched from the busy itinerant life of the evangelist. The Alline literary heritage consists of one closely reasoned and lengthy doctrinal treatise (*Two Mites Cast into the Offering of God*), one unclassifiable pamphlet (the *Anti-Traditionist*), three sermons, a volume of *Hymns and Spiritual Songs*, and an autobiography (*The Life and Journal of Henry Alline*). *Two Mites*, the *Anti-Traditionist*, the three sermons, and a short collection of hymns which has not survived, were all printed in Halifax between 1781 and 1783. The first two works, one of the sermons and a long selection of hymns (which was published posthumously) were reprinted in the United States under the auspices of the Freewill Baptists, and the hymns went through at least four American editions. The autobiography was also published after Alline's death in the United States, apparently from a manuscript which he left for this purpose. The tone and substance of Alline's writings are spiritual and pietistic, full of theological and doctrinal controversies which do not strike a responsive chord in the modern reader. It is doubtful whether the collected works of Henry Alline would ever become a modern best-seller. But within the confines of his own horizons and his own time, Alline was an intellectual and literary giant.

Following his formal schooling in Rhode Island, Henry Alline was forced to use his own devices to continue his education. His personality, his environment, and the times in which he lived clearly conditioned his commitment to the religious and spiritual issues which dominate his writings. But though Alline was self-made and self-educated to a large extent, the process of intellectual development did not occur in a complete void. As a guide to prose style and language, he had the greatest single standard in the English language: the King James version of the Bible. In terms of poetic form and content, he was familiar with the writings of John Milton, Alexander Pope, and John Pomfret, as well as the spiritual songs and hymns of Edward Young and Isaac Watts, the principal shapers of the modern hymnal tradition. He had also sampled a variety of religious writers, including Martin Luther and John Bunyan. Significantly, there is little indication of familiarity with the great doctrinal works of American Puritanism. Although Alline does cite books by Increase and Samuel Mather in his writings, these were works discussing Puritan church organization rather than theology. Some of Alline's writings, especially the *Anti-Traditionist*, show certain parallels with the metaphysical works of Jonathan Edwards, the great 18th-century New England

Puritan figure, but he gives no direct evidence of familiarity with
Edwardean thinking; it appears likely that the similarities are coin-
cidental rather than direct.

The writers and thinkers with whom Alline seems to have been
most familiar were English rather than American. They were generally men with a pietistic bent but lacking a systematic intellectual
position. Although Alline's basic doctrinal principles and attitudes
were clearly his own, one author did offer a theological formulation
which fitted his own predispositions: William Law, the great English
divine; on him Alline relied for the development of his own formal
ideology. Few contemporaries recognized Alline's debt to William
Law, and fewer still would have been favourably impressed by that
knowledge. Law, after all, was a non-juring Anglican excluded from
livings within his church, and was an ascetic mystic to boot.

What William Law would have thought of his Nova Scotian ad-
herent is difficult to say. On the other hand, Alline had much in common with Law, and responded favourably to the tenor of Law's writings. Both emphasized a thorough pietism bordering on asceticism;
for both men, the relationship with God was a daylong, lifelong matter. Neither married, and neither had any particular interest in
worldly affairs. Law rejected war because of the danger it brought to
unconverted soldiers, a sentiment with which Alline would probably
have agreed. Law had withdrawn from the world after refusing to
accept the Glorious Revolution in England in 1688, and he insisted
on loyalty to the ousted Stuart monarchs; Alline forsook the world
rather than take sides in the American Revolution in Nova Scotia.
But William Law became a recluse whose version of Christianity was
considered too perfectionist and difficult for the average man; he did
not attempt to convert others except through his writings, and his
thoughts turned increasingly inward toward mysticism. Although
Alline was equally mystical and ascetic, he attempted to combine

these tendencies with an enthusiastic evangelicalism. While Law the pietist clashed with John Wesley the evangelical in England, Alline in Nova Scotia wrestled with reconciling these two disparate positions. He was never entirely successful, and the effort undermined many of his evangelical successes, particularly when he adopted some of Law's later philosophy.

Although William Law communicated with the world only through his writings, these were both numerous and exceptionally well received in 18th-century England. Aside from various polemical writings on theological and religious issues of the time, Law's works can be divided into two parts. The first of them, written for the most part early in his career, were basically guidebooks to devotion. Two of these, *Christian Perfection* and *A Serious Call to a Devout and Holy Life*, were extremely popular with 18th-century pietists and evangelicals, and constituted one of the most important early influences on John Wesley, the founder of Methodism. They later served as basic texts for the Evangelical movement within the Anglican church at the end of the century. In his later years, however, Law came under the influence of the 16th-century German theosophist and mystic, Jacob Boehme, and many of his later works attempted to introduce Boehme's notions to the English audience. Evangelicals like John Wesley completely rejected Law's Behmenistic writings, which they considered overly confusing and mystical. Boehme's thinking as expounded by Law (and even Wesley admitted Law almost succeeded in making the ideas consistent and palatable) appealed greatly to Henry Alline, however, and the Nova Scotian employed this rather unorthodox system as the basis for his own doctrinal position and to attack the traditional Calvinism of most of his countrymen. Alline's personal experiences always had existential overtones, and his use of Behmenistic doctrines gave his writings a formal existential foundation.

Alline not only rejected the assumptions accepted by most Nova

Scotians, but he replaced them with an esoteric system almost totally incomprehensible to most of his audience, and certainly a tenuous one to maintain. In his writings, Alline's principal impediment was not, however, an absence of intellectual substance, but an insistence upon a position far beyond the understanding of the average Nova Scotian who responded positively to Alline's evangelical pietism while being repelled or confused by his doctrine. Alline's emphasis on the new birth, his Christian perfectionism, his rejection of earthly accomplishments, were themselves difficult enough to communicate to a community of 'sinners,' and his effort to give these in print a firm and viable theological basis verged on the disastrous particularly in terms of its reception by the public. His attempts to construct an alternative to Calvinistic theology as he understood it and his struggle to transform mysicism from a personal tendency into an element of formal theology met little favourable response from those receptive to his pietism and evangelical activities. Nova Scotians were willing to accept a certain undefinable deviation within traditional values, but not an open attack on the value system itself. This was probably most apparent with regard to his anti-Calvinism.

The traditional Calvinistic position as understood by most Nova Scotians – New Englander and Scots Presbyterian alike – was well stated in 1784 by Jonathan Scott, pastor of the church at Jebogue (Yarmouth) in a reply to Alline's *Two Mites*. Having clashed earlier with Alline the evangelist, Scott was obviously pleased to renew the conflict in *A Brief View of the Religious Tenets and Sentiments ... of Mr. Henry Alline*, which attacked Alline's religious position and focussed on his theology. Scott's Calvinistic God was at once omnipotent and inscrutable, except in so far as he chose to reveal himself through the scriptures. 'Out of his mere sovereign Will and good Pleasure, from Eternity,' God 'hath chosen and elected some men in Christ to everlasting Glory and Blessedness,' and condemned the remainder to eternal damnation. The fall of Adam placed all mankind in 'Trespasses and Sins,' and 'the Justice of God is *offended* by, and *incensed* against the *Sins of Man*.' According to Scott, the 'Revenging, incensed, vindictive Justice' of damnation does not make God unbenevolent, for it 'is an amiable, bright and glorious perfection in the most holy God.' To atone for the sins of men, Christ 'made his Life a Sacrifice to the offended, revenging Justice of God,' and 'fully satisfied' this justice for 'those who truely believe on his Name, at all Times even to the End of the World.' Of course, atonement was limited, for only those who had been unconditionally elected and predestined by God could hope to be saved. Sinners 'have not Power to quicken themselves, but are dependent on a sovereign God for such Mercy.'[1] Any attempt to assign to the sinner an initial freedom to act on his own behalf for salvation or to make anyone eligible for God's grace was rejected by Calvinists like Scott as, in the epithet of the time, 'Arminianism.'

Jonathan Scott was no reactionary. His defence of Calvinism not only ranged widely in the writings of the Puritan fathers, but also relied heavily on the recent restatement of Calvinistic dogma by the great New England theologian, Jonathan Edwards. Nevertheless, Scott not only accepted the 'Five Points of Calvinism' as enunciated by the Synod of Dort (1618–1619) – unconditional election, limited atonement, total depravity, irresistible grace, and the perseverance of the saints – but also insisted on a vengeful, arbitrary, and selective God. Against this view of the Deity, particularly, Henry Alline rebelled.

The refusal to accept the doctrines of Calvinism was in part a result of Alline's own experience of conversion. He had discovered at that time that God was not only benevolent but loving, and felt that, as a sinner, he had turned to God of his own free will. Alline had made the 'decision for Christ' unaided by outside human factors, and this fact seemed to increase the degree of responsibility which he alone had for the action. As has already been noted, Alline's experience was quite compatible with orthodox Calvinism; it all depended on how one interpreted the process of the extension of grace by God and the response of the individual to this offer. By itself, his conversion did not inevitably lead to an anti-Calvinistic position. But when Alline attempted to fit this conversion into the evangelical message which he began to preach to Nova Scotians, the result was a reaction against orthodox dogma.

Strict Calvinism and evangelical revivalism have always been uneasy partners. If only a few men are unconditionally elected and most are unconditionally consigned to damnation, and if the power to 'quicken' comes from God only to those previously chosen, the scope of action for the revivalist becomes extremely limited. He can do no more than assist those few who have already been foreordained to be awakened by God and cannot hope to have any effect on the great mass of sinful humanity. Evangelical revivalism, by its very nature, tends to universalism (all men can be saved) and arminianism (salvation comes through an effort of will by man). Most great revivalists have rejected or at least largely reinterpreted orthodox Calvinist doctrine. Among major revivals, only the Great Awakening in New England from 1740 to 1745 occurred in a basically Calvinistic framework, and this was a result of the peculiar version of Calvinism prevalent in New England at the time combined with a relative absence of Calvinistic doctrine in the preaching of the itinerant evangelists. Men like George Whitefield, Gilbert Tennent, and Eleazer Wheelock may have been Calvinists, but their revival sermons blithely ignored questions of dogma. Jonathan Edwards maintained a strict Calvinism, but was not really an itinerant or a successful evangelical. Totally divorced from New England theology, Henry Alline naturally found himself tending toward universalism and arminianism, and he sought a consistent doctrinal system in which to place these tendencies. This he found in the writings of William Law.

The major message of Law was that 'God is Love.' But if the deity is benevolent, how could evil enter into the universe? Law answered this question by emphasizing that the perfect and good qualities of God may become imperfect and evil in limited and finite creatures. He postulated a 'pre-Creation' of angels existing in heavily light and love. The angels revolted from God of their own free will, and their fall produced the world, for out of their ruined, angelic kingdom God created the world and man. Adam, like the angels, fell because of God's gift of free will. When man, the breath of God, began to will and desire contrary to the deity, he became an earthly creature and, in effect, died. Law saw this interpretation of the fall as consistent with the great truth that God is Love, and also as an explanation of original sin and sinful man. How could earthly, sinful, dead Adam beget anything other than children of the same nature and condition with himself? Man could be restored only by a new birth – by having God rekindle the divine life. This was the function of Jesus, the second Adam, and his redemption was universal. The atonement of Christ extinguished sin in the Creature, and Jesus was the light of all men who are by free grace of God made sons of the second Adam; all men share in Christ's rebirth. Christ's suffering made all men eligible for salvation, and God had granted all men free will. Therefore, all men could be saved, although the process of rebirth was not an easy one. Calvinism was an abomination to William Law, and his theological system totally overturned the teachings of the Geneva reformer and his followers.

Most of the basic principles of Law were repeated and expanded by Henry Alline in his major work of systematic theology, *Two Mites Cast into the Offering of God*. Alline in his preface admitted that the reader might find 'some things in these few lines, that may appear new, and different from what you have been taught,' and frankly indicated his objections to traditional dogma.[2] He warned that though he had made use of some writers, he did not necessarily approve all their principles. His teaching was eclectic, though grounded in the word of God, the scriptures. The warning was probably intended to protect Alline against accusations of being a slavish disciple of Law, but proved irrelevant, since among his contemporaries only John Wesley (who had been sent Alline's works by the Nova Scotia Methodist, William Black) appears to have recognized Alline's debt to Law. Alline's use of Law was clearly selective, and the Nova Scotian in a variety of ways made the position his own. He did not rely heavily on citations to the authority of Law or any other theologian (partly because he wrote 'on the road' removed from any book collections), he translated those principles he adopted into a language he hoped would be comprehensible to Nova Scotians, and he grounded his argument in scripture and common sense. Even his references to scripture were frequently cryptic and incomplete, and Alline's principal didactic device was the everyday metaphor and simile following from what he regarded as assumptions acceptable to all reasonable men: the benevolence of God and the free will of man.

Alline began his exposition of systematic doctrine in *Two Mites* with a statement of his two major insights. God is good, and man himself is responsible for the fall from grace (and hence is capable of recovering redemption). He left no doubt from the very beginning of this work that his major attack would be on Calvinism. God created man according to His own nature as an intelligent being 'capable of acting as a free Agent.' To claim that the fall was foreordained was to charge sin upon God, who is not inscrutable. All laws, decrees, or statutes, in heaven, earth, or hell, are a reflection of God's divine nature, and is it not more reasonable, scriptural, and Christian to believe that God acts from love rather than vindictiveness? Calvinist writings are 'of no more worth than so many old Almanacks.' If God is not vengeful, arbitrary, and unknowable, so man is not powerless to act on his own behalf. Man is in a state of probation, and 'salvation and damnation originates here at your own door,' with 'no bar between you and redeeming love, but what is in your own breast, held up of choice.'[3] In an attack on the inconsistency of evangelical Calvinism, Alline pointed out that while Calvinists preached there is room for all, their doctrine of election belied the claim.

With his major themes clearly enunciated, Alline then moved on to attempt to construct a coherent doctrinal system which supported his position. The fall of Adam came not because of eating an apple or through the imposition of God's will; God did not kill or threaten to kill Adam for eating the apple, but simply warned of the consequences which would ensure from a separation from Him. Man fell of his own volition, with his collective free will embodied in one being – Adam. Alline insisted he did not reject original sin, for there could be no doubt that the 'whole race of mankind are in a fallen state of sin and misery,' but he argued against the common views of the fall and the 'imputation' of sin to Adam's descendants. When God created man, he created *all* mankind, and all men (as embodied in Adam) were guilty of breaking the communication of the divine light and love of God. To wait for election is foolish, since it will never come; all men fell into an equal condition, and all had the same opportunity for salvation – to fly to the lamb of God, 'whose infinite love waits to redeem you out of your own nature and restore you to his.' God stooped to redeem sinners through Christ, stepping down into the nature of man so 'as to become capable of his suffering and death for the fallen world.' God did this not 'to appease any vindictive wrath, or satisfy any incensed justice in the deity but to die wholly in, and for, the fallen race; to remove wrath and hell and ten thousand disorders from them.'[4]

All mankind was equally sinful, and all mankind can be saved. To this extent Alline was a universalist. God offered redemption to 'all that will and can be redeemed out of the world.' But not all would be saved, because not all would experience a 'divine change of heart.' Alline insisted that he did not deny the doctrine of election; he simply objected to the concept that God did the electing. 'If there is any cause, why some are more choaked with thorns, and tied down to this bestial world, than others, the cause must certainly be found in man, and not in the hands of God.' It was man who built up 'walls of separation between God' and his soul, and then charged God with being the cause of his destruction. Like most successful evangelists, Alline saw salvation coming when man 'determined to cast himself at his feet, and trust wholly to his mercy, and free grace for salvation; and cries out with the trembling leper, *Lord if thou wilt!*"[5]

Alline's overt attack on Calvinism undoubtedly cost him a good deal of support from within the province, for New Englanders and Scottish Presbyterians had grown up with the doctrine since their childhood. Most, if not all, of the churches which he founded were basically Calvinistic in their 'Articles of Faith.' Indeed, the Cornwallis church, embodied in 1778 with Alline present – one of the churches which ordained him to the ministry – drew up a statement of belief which denied almost in its entirety his own doctrinal position. Although Cornwallis never repudiated him, another of his sponsoring churches – the Horton Baptist Church – did so immediately after the publication of *Two Mites*. On 3 February 1781 the Horton church called for 'a general meeting of the churches that was assisting in the ordination of Mr. Henry Alline,' partly because of his position 'concerning the ordinance of Baptism' and partly because of 'some of his Doctrine.' Alline and the other churches refused to meet, and on 2 April 1781 the Horton church admonished 'our Brother Henry Alline in the first place for paying no regard to the Request of the Church and for Publishing Erronious principles in print.'[6] Similarly, in Liverpool, Simeon Perkins, the town's leading citizen, turned against Alline, probably after reading *Two Mites*.[7] In his 1784 attack on Alline, Jonathan Scott undoubtedly sensed the undercurrent of discontent with Alline's 'doctrine' and hit hard at his anti-Calvinism, obviously anticipating that a thorough exposure of the evangelist's break with tradition would turn many against him. In the long run it undoubtedly did, and the successful heirs of Alline's evangelical thrust were the Baptists, whose position was generally Calvinistic in nature.

If Alline produced disenchantment because of his attack on Calvinism, at least this was a result of a point of view clearly expounded. The opening chapters of *Two Mites* were Alline's clearest and most carefully reasoned statements. Unfortunately, in the concluding pages of *Two Mites*, in his pamphlet the *Anti-Traditionist*, and scattered throughout his published sermons was a far less rational current of metaphysical mysticism which was totally incomprehensible to the average reader. It was this underlying theme in his writings which led John Wesley to comment that Alline 'is very far from being a man of sound understanding; but he has been dabbling in Mystical writers, in matters which are too high for him, far above his comprehension. I dare not waste my time upon such miserable jargon.'[8] Wesley might not agree with Alline's anti-Calvinistic position, but he could not dismiss the first hundred pages of *Two Mites* as 'miserable jargon.' Much of Alline's other published writing was nevertheless open to the charge of confusing abstruseness. He was attempting to come to grips with the important intellectual and philosophical issues of his time, however, and the position which he expounded resembled, in broad outline, that of William Law (from whom much of it was taken) and Jonathan Edwards.

Occasional glimpses of Alline's views intruded even in the earlier pages of *Two Mites*, but they were undeveloped and the reader could pass them over as essentially unnecessary to the argument. He spoke briefly in chapter 2 ('On God's Decrees and Man's fall not Decreed') of the 'everlasting Outbirth,' an emanation from God of an eternal nature which transcended the created universe, but he did not expand the concept at this point. The Outbirth was returned to in the *Anti-Traditionist*, however, as Alline attempted to explain 'the Design and Nature of Creation,' the first attempt by a Canadian writer in English to wrestle with this complex metaphysical question.

Alline in *Two Mites* had insisted that God could be comprehended by man; in the *Anti-Traditionist* he emphasized that He 'is, ever was, and forever will be incomprehensible.' Nevertheless, Henry Alline would 'endeavour to discover something of the Certainty, consistency, and Nature of an infinite, beginning, ever-lasting, self-existent and Supreme Being.' Since it was axiomatic that nothing comes into existence from 'nothing or chance,' this not only demonstrated a 'first Cause' but one 'possessed of an infinite unbeginning self-necessary Source of Life.' All God's actions 'manifest his Glory, Goodness, Happiness,' and he created 'wholly from the View and Enjoyment of himself.'[9] This particular view of God's reasons for creation has a good deal in common with that advanced by Jonathan Edwards a quarter-century earlier. But Alline's subsequent exposition makes it clear that his source was the Law-Boehme tradition rather than that of Edwards, for he then proposed an existential angelic system which existed before the physical universe was created. Both systems were not really creations, but rather an 'Outbirth,' a manifestation of God's indwelling presence in everything. The fall of the angels from God created the world, which was 'corporeal' rather than ethereal. For Alline, the corporeal physical universe is 'fallen Nature interposed,' with the implication that the material world is distinctly inferior to the spiritual in an actual rather than a symbolic sense.[10] This position was as close to mysticism as any Protestant could possibly get, and led Alline to favour a severe asceticism as well.

For Alline, moreover, Eve (woman) was not responsible for the fall but was rather a consequence of it. Man as originally 'created' was sexless, but 'when this innumerable Throng had broke off from the Triune Father, they thereby broke up and made a Division among themselves, and in their own Male and Femal [*sic*] Powers, not only at Enmity against God; and at War one with another, but each one having that Triune Life broke up at War and with a Torment to himself.' Redemption comes only through a reunion of the Creature with God, in which the male and the female will again 'be as much and undividedly one as he and his Father.'[11] Alline here found a doctrinal justification for his personal decision to resist the wiles of women.

Because Alline equated the material universe and fallen nature, the resurrection for him became spiritual and mystical rather than physical. Much of his writing, in the concluding chapters of *Two Mites*, in the *Anti-Traditionist*, and in the sermons, was devoted to detailed descriptions of the resurrection and the day of judgement. 'Hellfire and brimstone' eschatology was part of the stock-in-trade of most revivalists, but for Alline the day of judgement was more than simply a persuasive device. It was a genuine mystical vision. His language in these passages became coloured and vivid:

> The seas roar, the rocks melt, the earth trembles,
> the thunders rattle, lightnings play; earthquakes
> rend; inundations overflow; houses burn; pyramids
> reel; villages, towns and kingdoms sink; while
> burning hills exceed mount Aetna's or Visuvius' [*sic*]
> flames; the graves open; the dead arise the
> quick are changed; and first the saints appear.
> ... What awful throes! What heart rending
> groans and cheerful shouts are now heard thro'
> the promiscuous and innumerable throngs![12]

Throughout his eschatological passages, the reader must sense that

Alline wrote as an eye-witness reporter, and in more than one place in his works are references to his own visions and experiences. Henry Alline was not imagining but describing.

The passages exemplary of Alline's mystical streak at its most compelling are probably not to be found in his published writings, either in the metaphysical or in the eschatological sections. They must instead be sought in private correspondence, only a few pieces of which have survived. When Alline attempted to fit mysticism into a theological system he sounded forced and confused, and was open to the charge levelled against him by Jonathan Scott that he sought to appeal to the 'Passions of the Reader, especially the young, ignorant and inconsistent, who are influenced more by the Sound and Gingle of the words.'[13] But Alline's mysticism was considerably more than a rhetorical trick and in several unpublished letters he produced some fine and moving passages of religious literature. From Argyle, for example, in 1782 he wrote:

> And O let me intreat a people near my heart to keep
> near your Glorious Leader; that you may be both
> happy, and usefull; I know there is no need of
> Telling you he is All in All, and that without
> him all is Vanity and vexation of Spirit; O then
> what can possibly find place in your souls but
> Jesus that infinite Lover! Can fears, or frowns,
> prosperity or adversity, Crowns and Kingdoms, Life
> or Death break your hold, or Steal your affections
> from him that is so strong, so worthy of your Love
> who Bought you so dear? ... O the unspeakable
> happiness those must enjoy who walk near the lovely
> Jesus! Surely it must be great indeed when one
> Who Travels at so vast a distance As I do, Enjoy so
> much from the Glimmering Rays, that I now and then
> Attain of the hem of his Garment.[14]

In such passages Henry Alline was wholly himself, and was a far more attractive figure than in his self-conscious published writings. His involved mystical doctrines certainly repelled the non-nonsense Methodists, and probably threw a good many converts into their camp, particularly after his death.

Related to Alline's mysticism was a strong current of asceticism. Alline's anti-Calvinism was comprehensible and convincing, though it flew in the face of traditional beliefs. His mysticism was esoteric and confusing to most Nova Scotians. The difficulty with his asceticism was that it was too demanding and unrealistic an ethic for a leader of a potential mass movement to espouse. Intellectually, Alline's almost medieval monasticism was a logical conclusion of his mystical view of the material world as fallen nature, which must be transcended by the new birth into reunion with God. The human body was corporeal and sinful by nature, and had to be battled against by the 'inmost soul, or immortal mind.' Alline called for 'the mortification of the old man,' for 'as you love your own soul, keep under your body.'[15] It was in an effort to 'starve the old man' that he opposed 'frolicking,' drinking, horse-racing, profanity, and other forms of human 'wickedness.' Unlike later opponents of 'sin,' he did not hold that the body was a temple of God that must be kept pure, but rather that material existence was by definition an iniquity which must be overcome. Nova Scotia was not an unusually corrupt society so much as Alline's standards were extremely high. But part of his social ethic involved the foresaking of all worldly pleasures – however innocent appearing to most of the populace – and he himself set the example, hard as it was to follow.

To view Alline as preaching nothing more than a process of bodily self-flagellation is really to miss the widespread popular appeal and significance of his message in Nova Scotia during the American Revolution. His rejection of the world fitted into the political and social conditions of the time, and scattered throughout his writings is not only an 'otherworldly' asceticism, but an ethical appeal which was, in its own way, revolutionary. Traditional Calvinists objected to his theology, evangelical Methodists to his mysticism, but both these groups were by and large outside positions of power and authority in the province. The Anglican establishment in Nova Scotia, however, came to view the "Allinites" as a definite threat to its position. In the short run, Alline contributed to keeping Nova Scotia quiet during the trying years of Revolution. But in the long run, the implications of his ethical position were dangerous to the authorities, for he emphasized a levelling egalitarianism which rejected instituted government in favour of what can probably best be described as the self-government of the godly.

Egalitarianism was an integral part of Alline's evangelical message, since the Redeemer offered himself to 'any man, Jew or Gentile, bond or free, male or female, old or young, rich or poor, none excepted.' All mankind was capable of salvation, for there was no election of the saints by God but rather a process of self-selection. Alline was not content with a simple universalist message, however, and he made a special appeal to the disinherited. This involved in part a denial that 'earthly dignity, the esteem of man or a conspicuous station in the world' made a man of God, and in part a positive implication that the spirit of Christ is more likely to be found 'among the most poor and despicable people on the earth.' In his account of the day of judgement he included among the 'ungodly' not only 'murderers, whoremongers and adulterers,' but 'kings, princes and monarchs.' He did not insist that all monarchs were ungodly but simply that they would have no special privileges on the day of judgement. And he was willing to push his teaching to its ultimate conclusion, emphasizing that Christ commanded his followers 'to salute no man by the way.'[16]

Along with his levelling message, which was bound to have a powerful appeal in a newly settled back-country society such as that in Nova Scotia, was an anti-militaristic note which found fertile soil in the province. For Alline, 'wars and rumours of war, yea the most inhumane wars spreading desolation through the world like a flood' were signals of the approaching day of judgement. In a 1782 sermon at Liverpool, he gave thanks for the absence of war in Nova Scotia, but insisted that this was not 'because of the cleaness [*sic*] of our hands, or past righteousness: for surely we have not only had our hands equally engaged in the sins that have incurred the lamentable disorder; but have likewise perpetrated the same crimes.'[17] Alline indicated a continuing suspicion that those in military service were particularly dissolute and sinful, although he offered them the message of redemption.

Understandably, the Anglican authorities came to see a revolutionary movement in the New-Light revival begun by Alline. It has been fashionable to see Anglican fears as unwarranted, but the establishment was not being overly sensitive. The government of Nova Scotia, emphasizing as it did loyalty to the monarchy and the need for a deferential social order, in which the lower classes would consent to being governed by their betters, was quite perceptive in its frequently voiced suspicions that 'the conductors of these people are engaged in the general plan of *a total revolution in religious and civil government*.'[18] Henry Alline never attacked the established Anglican Church nor did he explicitly preach a doctrine of the separation of church or state, but this was because he had more important things to do in his short ministry. He made it quite clear to civil leaders, however, that 'great is the influence of men in your state; and as great when your ways are perverse and your examples ungodly.'[19] Throughout his career, Alline insisted on a withdrawal from 'this ensnaring world' by true Christians, for 'you have no continuing city here.'[20] But the anti-authoritarian levelling implications of his doctrine and ethic, com-

bined with the democratic nature of church government as he
expounded it, were capable of producing a revolutionary ideology, as
had occurred in the thirteen colonies to the south of Nova Scotia.
That Canada's evangelical pietism never became revolutionary is to
be attributed to his successors and not to Alline himself.

With all Alline's writings, one is struck by the speed with which
they were forgotten and their lack of deep impact upon the society in
which they were written. Even his hymns, so popular in their own
time that they were laboriously copied out by hand and approved
even by his opponents, have long since ceased to be part of Canada's
hymnology. Ironically, the only Alline hymn which remained in
hymnals long beyond his death was attributed to someone else. As was
the case with his doctrinal principles, the hymns remained important
far longer and were more influential in the United States than in
Alline's native land.

It is frequently difficult to explain why any figure sinks into obscurity. In the case of Alline, however, several factors seem important.
In the first place, his writings were ignored by his contemporaries in
British North America because existential mysticism was too revision-
ist and too intellectualized to suit the society of the time. His evangelical successors, the Calvinistic Baptists and the Methodists, were
more interested in revivalism than in setting down in print the doctrine on which it was based. After Alline's death, evangelical pietism
in the Maritimes ignored, perhaps even refused to enter, the area of
the printed word for nearly half a century. By the time pietists again
turned to publishing their ideas, Alline's intellectual position was little
more than an historical curiosity. But many individuals who were
neglected by their immediate descendants have been resurrected and
admired by subsequent generations. That this has not happened with
Henry Alline is a result of other factors built into the historical development of Canada. Alline devoted his life to goals with which our

modern secular society is distinctly out of sympathy, and he pursued them in a region which most Canadians have come to regard as of only secondary importance to the nation. The obscurity of Henry Alline is a measure of the failure of most Canadians to move beyond the study of politics in central Canada in the search for their heritage.

5

A Burning and Shining Light, and Justly Esteemed the Apostle of Nova Scotia

Late in 1783 the dying Henry Alline resolutely set forth to New England, insisting 'I would go and proclaim my Master's name, where I never had preached, as long as I could ride or stand, if it was even to the last expiring breath.'[1] He quite literally lived up to this promise, preaching his last sermon only a week before his death. What impelled Alline to leave the Maritimes for the United States? Perhaps, as has recently been suggested, he felt it the duty of an awakened Nova Scotia to bring the gospel to a fallen New England.[2] But there is little evidence that Alline saw the Americans in any more dire need of awakening than the population of what remained of Britain's American empire, or that he felt any special sense of mission to the United States. Before 1783 (the year in which Britain by treaty formally recognized the independence of the United States) a journey there might have been dangerous and difficult. If one examines Alline's constantly widening evangelical territory it becomes obvious that the coming of political peace virtually coincided with that point at which his circuit reached the borders of the United States. He was continually expanding his mission to reach a new audience ('where I never had preached') and it was the Americans' turn.

Although the bulk of his labours had been in Maritime Canada, Alline died in North-Hampton, New Hampshire, at the home of David McClure, a minister of the Calvinistic Puritan establishment of New England against which Alline had battled most of his adult life. His funeral was executed by a Puritan church, his corpse born to its grave by Puritan ministers (including Seth Noble, formerly of Maugerfield), and he was interred in a burying yard surrounded by orthodox Calvinists. Despite the irony surrounding his death and burial, it was entirely fitting that the location should not be in Nova Scotia but in coastal New Hampshire, for this symbolized the future direction of Alline's immediate influence. His work in the Maritimes had been finished, and his mission would live on through the efforts of Benjamin Randall of Portsmouth, New Hampshire (a few miles north of North-Hampton), who founded the Freewill Baptist movement in the United States.

As the epitaph on Alline's gravestone recorded, 'He was a burning and shining Light, and was justly esteemed the apostle of Nova Scotia.'[3] But most of the churches which Alline had founded in Nova Scotia and New Brunswick either collapsed or went over to the Baptists, who rejected his anti-Calvinistic theology and his attempts to open communion to all who had experienced the new birth. Almost all the succeeding generation of Baptist ministers had their souls first stirred by Alline, but they were in the end converted by others. Both his concrete accomplishments and his writings were forgotten.

Yet to write Alline off as a failure would be a mistake. His life as an evangelical missionary was short, but it encompassed a crucial period in the history of the Maritimes; he was not only a creature of his age, but he played an important role in it as well. He symbolized the difficulties which New Englanders faced in Nova Scotia during the era of the American Revolution, and in addition he offered a viable alternative to political involvement and earthly discontent. The alternative, like Alline himself, was a complex one, at one time anti-British and anti-American, radical and counter-revolutionary. His message was peculiarly Nova Scotian, and it had a special relevance in the years of political crisis which the province faced. In a sense, this helps explain the rapid descent of his reputation into oblivion: conditions after 1784 altered greatly, but he did not live to change with the times.

Finally, however much Alline was a product of his age, he was also a product of the desire of man throughout most of history for closer communion with his Creator. The part of Alline's message that was exclusively and unmistakably his may have had a short life, but the general movement of evangelical pietism which he sparked in Canada survived, prospered, and grew to become a basic component of the

Canadian ethos and way of life until well into the present century. The ideals of pietism do not appeal to most members of modern society, and it must be admitted that what has longest survived of pietism is not the deep concern for one's own relationship with God but rather a compulsive attempt to regulate the external behaviour of others. Henry Alline did not make the mistake of confusing moral regulation with what he considered to be the core of Christianity – love of God. Alline may have opposed sin, but he would not necessarily have supported legislation to curtail it. Indeed, the various 'blue laws' which remain in Canada as a principal heritage of pietism would probably have been openly deplored by Alline and his generation, since their ethic stressed individual reform through a closer communion with God rather than corporate or governmental action.

Although Alline might not have agreed with subsequent legislation taken in the name of Christian piety, he was still responsible for introducing into Canada pietistic ways of viewing the world and evangelical means of spreading the gospel. These were ideally suited to a pioneer country. For as long as the nation had a frontier, evangelical pietism would remain a valid approach to man's search for a meaningful relationship with God.

NOTES

CHAPTER ONE

1 Genealogies of the Alline family are given in John V. Duncanson, *Falmouth – A New England Township in Nova Scotia 1760–1965* (Windsor, Ont., 1965), pp. 167–168. Spelling of the name in contemporary documents is usually either 'Allin' or 'Allen,' which suggests that it is to be pronounced to rhyme with 'win' not 'wine.'

2 Henry Alline, *The Life and Journal of the Rev. Mr. Henry Alline* (Boston 1806), p. 7

3 Alline, *Life and Journal*, p. 3

4 Otis Little, *A Geographical History of Nova Scotia* (London 1749), pp. 22–23

5 *Boston Gazette*, 12 October 1758

6 This proclamation is reprinted in full in John Bourinot, 'Builders of Nova Scotia: A Historical Review' (Royal Society of Canada, *Transactions*, 1899, pp. 136–137).

7 Alline, *Life and Journal*, p. 7

8 *Ibid.*

9 Public Archives of Nova Scotia, vol. 211, 24 July 1762

10 Quoted in K. R. Williams, 'Social Conditions in Nova Scotia 1749–1783' (unpublished M.A. thesis, McGill University, 1936), p. 150.

11 Quoted in Williams, 'Social Conditions,' p. 151.

12 John Robinson and Thomas Rispin, *Journey through Nova-Scotia containing a particular Account of the Country and its Inhabitants* (York 1774), reprinted in *Report of the Board of Trustees of the Public Archives of Nova Scotia* (1944), p. 49.

13 Robinson and Rispin, *Journey*, pp. 49–50

14 Carl Bridenbaugh, ed., 'Patrick M' Robert's *Tour through Part of the North Provinces of America*' (*Pennsylvania Magazine of History and Biography*, LIX, 1935, 153–155)

15 Hon. Alexander Grant to Rev. Ezra Stiles, May 1760, reprinted in George S. Brown, *Yarmouth, Nova Scotia* (Boston 1888), p. 128.

16 *Nova Scotia Chronicle and Weekly Advertiser*, 16 January 1770

17 Joseph Bennett to SPG, 29 August 1769, Transcripts of Papers of the Society for the Propagation of the Gospel in Foreign Parts, Public Archives of Canada, B. 25, p. 370

CHAPTER TWO

1 Alline, *Life and Journal*, p. 20
2 Alline, *Life and Journal*, p. 9
3 Edmund S. Morgan, *Visible Saints: The History of a Puritan Idea* (New York 1963), p. 67
4 Morgan, *Visible Saints*, p. 68
5 Alline, *Life and Journal*, pp. 3–4, 4–5, 6
6 Alline, *Life and Journal*, pp. 10, 12–13, 16–17, 17–19
7 Alline, *Life and Journal*, pp. 20–22
8 Alline, *Life and Journal*, pp. 23–24
9 Alline, *Life and Journal*, pp. 24–31
10 Alline, *Life and Journal*, pp. 31–39
11 Alline, *Life and Journal*, p. 4
12 Duncanson, *Falmouth*, p. 274
13 Alline, *Life and Journal*, pp. 36–37
14 Alline, *Life and Journal*, p. 41
15 Alline, *Life and Journal*, p. 42
16 Alline, *Life and Journal*, pp. 42–43
17 Alline, *Life and Journal*, p. 44
18 Quoted in John B. Brebner, *The Neutral Yankees of Nova Scotia: A Marginal Colony during the Revolutionary Years* (New York 1937), pp. 309–310.
19 Alline, *Life and Journal*, pp. 45–47

CHAPTER THREE

1 A 'Mrs. Fox' of Horton, quoted by W. B. Bezanson, *The Romance of Religion: A Sketch of the Life of Henry Alline in the Pioneer Days of the Maritime Provinces* (Kentville 1927), p. 15.
2 Brebner, *Neutral Yankees*, p. 324
3 Alline, *Life and Journal*, p. 47
4 Alline, *Life and Journal*, p. 70, see below, p. 69
5 Alline, *Life and Journal*, p. 151
6 Alline, *Life and Journal*, p. 109
7 Joseph Crandall, 'Autobiography' (Maritime Baptist Historical Collection, Acadia University, Wolfville, Nova Scotia), p. 1
8 Alline, *Life and Journal*, p. 147
9 Henry Alline, *Hymns and Spiritual Songs* (several editions)
10 Alline, *A Court for the Trial of Anti-Traditionist* (n.p., n.d.), p. 13

11 Personal letters of Henry Alline *et al.* (Maritime Baptist Historical Collection)
12 Alline, *Life and Journal*, p. 145
13 Alline, *Life and Journal*, p. 167
14 See Charles Bruce Fergusson, ed., *The Life of Jonathan Scott* (Halifax 1960) and Earl B. Eddy, 'The Uncrowned Bishop of Congregationalism: The Story of Jonathan Scott,' (Committee of Archives of the United Church of Canada, *Bulletin*, IX, 1956, 25–34.
15 Alline, *Life and Journal*, p. 151
16 Scott, *A Brief View of the Religious Tenets and Sentiments ... of Mr. Henry Alline* (Halifax 1784), pp. 221–224
17 Alline, *Life and Journal*, p. 50
18 Matthew Richey, *A Memoir of the Late Rev. William Black, Wesleyan Minister* (Halifax 1839), pp. 107–108
19 Alline, *Life and Journal*, pp. 53, 160–162
20 Jonathan Scott, *A Brief View*, p. 223
21 Henry Alline, *Two Mites Cast Into the Offering of God, for the Benefit of Mankind* (Dover, N.H., 1804), 234–235
22 Alline, *Two Mites*, 109, 127, 144, 148–149, 155, 124
23 Alline, *Two Mites*, pp. 248–249
24 Alline, *Life and Journal*, pp. 117–118
25 For alternative interpretations of the Nova Scotia Awakening to the one which follows, see M. W. Armstrong, 'Neutrality and Religion in Revolutionary Nova Scotia,' *New England Quarterly*, XIX (1946), 50–62; and George Rawlyk and Gordon Stewart, 'Nova Scotia's Sense of Mission,' *Histoire sociale/Social History*, number 2 (November 1968), pp. 5–17.
26 D. C. Harvey, ed., *Journeys to the Island of St. John* (Toronto 1955), p. 39
27 The 'Articles of Faith and practice with the Covenant that is confessed by the Church of Christ in Cornwallis this 15th day of July One Thousand, Seven Hundred and Seventy Eight' (Cornwallis Church Records, Maritime Baptist Historical Collection) offer the best evidence of church practice in Allinite churches. Quotations in the remainder of this chapter come from this covenant, unless otherwise noted.
28 Alline, *Life and Journal*, p. 75
29 Alline, *Life and Journal*, p. 179

CHAPTER FOUR

1 Scott, *A Brief View*, pp, 27, 61, 67, 75–77, 31
2 Alline, *Two Mites*, pp. iii–iv

3 Alline, *Two Mites*, pp. 2, 9, 14, 23
4 Alline, *Two Mites*, pp. 37, 53, 68, 72
5 Alline, *Two Mites*, pp. 98, 103, 88
6 Horton Church Records (Maritime Baptist Historical Collection), pp. 28–31
7 Perkins, *Diary*, II, 222
8 John Telford, ed., *The Letters of the Rev. John Wesley*, VII (London 1931), p. 182
9 Alline, *A Court for the Trial of Anti-Traditionist*, pp. 10, 15–17
10 Alline, *Anti-Traditionist*, pp. 23–36
11 Alline, *Anti-Traditionist*, pp. 37–38
12 Alline, *Two Mites*, pp. 194–195
13 Scott, *A Brief View*, p. 168
14 Henry Alline to 'my Dear fellow pilgrims for the promis'd Land,' 16 October 1782 (Maritime Baptist Historical Collection)
15 Alline, *Two Mites*, pp. 96–97
16 Alline, *Two Mites*, pp. 86, 109, 205–206, 245
17 Alline, *A Sermon on a Day of Thanksgiving Preached at Liverpool* (Halifax, n.d.), p. 22. This statement seems the clearest evidence that Alline did not see Nova Scotia as being particularly favoured by God, as Rawlyk and Stewart have argued.
18 J. M. Bumsted, 'Church and State in Maritime Canada, 1749–1807' (Canadian Historical Association, *Historical Papers*, 1968, p. 56)
19 Alline, *Liverpool Sermon*, p. 25
20 Alline, *Two Mites*, pp. 243, 245

CHAPTER FIVE

1 Alline, *Life and Journal*, p. 171
2 Rawlyk and Stewart, 'Nova Scotia's Sense of Mission'
3 An illustration of the gravestone is reproduced in Duncanson, *Falmouth*, p. 39.

BIBLIOGRAPHY

Henry Alline published five works within his own lifetime. These were: *Two Mites on Some of the Most Important and much disputed Points of Divinity* ... (Halifax 1781); *A Court for the Trial of Anti-Traditionist* (no date, no place, but probably Halifax 1783); *Sermon Preached to, and at the Request, of a Religious Society of Young Men United and Engaged for the Maintaining and Enjoying of Religious Worship in Liverpool, on the 19th November, 1782* (Halifax, no date, but probably 1783); *A Sermon on a Day of Thanksgiving Preached at Liverpool, By Henry Alline. On the 21st, of November 1782* (Halifax, no date, but probably 1783); and *A Sermon Preached on the 19th of February 1783 at Fort-Midway* (Halifax, no date, but probably 1783). The first item was reprinted "With Some Amendments by Benjamin Randal" and retitled *Two Mites, Cast into the Offering of God, for the Benefit of Mankind* (Dover, New Hampshire, 1804). The reprinting differs from the 1781 edition only in the omission of a few paragraphs, for reasons which appear inexplicable. The *Anti-Traditionist* was reprinted at Dover in 1797, and the Fort-Midway sermon (retitled *A Gospel Call to Sinners!*) was reprinted in Newburyport, Massachusetts, in 1795. In addition to these works, *The Life and Journal of the Rev. Mr. Henry Alline* (Boston 1806) and Alline's *Hymns and Spiritual Songs* (four editions: Boston 1786; Dover, New Hampshire, 1795 and 1797; and Stonington-Port, Connecticut, 1802) appeared after his death, apparently from manuscripts which Alline left in charge of the Reverend David McClure, at whose house he died in 1784.

Besides the published writings, there are a few Alline items in manuscript at the Maritime Baptist Historical Collection, Acadia University, Wolfville, Nova Scotia. A manuscript copy of *The Life and Journal* purportedly in Alline's hand is in this collection, but the writing appears insead to be that of McClure, for a section in the same hand as the entire manuscript was added describing Alline's death and funeral. The collection does include the manuscript – in Alline's writing – of *Two Mites*. Only one of a number of Alline letters ('To the gospel church at Argyle' which still bears the address of Mr. John Spinney 'at Argyle' and the original seal) is definitely in Alline's handwriting, and no other pieces in the collection except *Two Mites* appear to be originals. Nevertheless, this collection (calendared in *A Catalogue of the Maritime Baptist Historical Collection in the Library of Acadia University*, available from the Library) is the richest and almost only source for the New-Light/Baptist movement in the Maritimes, and I have relied upon it heavily.

Three full-length biographical studies of Alline have been undertaken previous to this one. Only W. B. Bezanson, *The Romance of Religion: A Sketch of the Life of Henry Alline* (Kentville, NS, 1927) has been published. But see also Earl W. Eldridge, 'Henry Alline: The Apostle of Nova Scotia' (unpublished BD thesis, Andover-Newton Theological School, 1948), and George A. Morrison, 'Henry Alline – Man of Conflict' (unpublished BD thesis, Acadia University, 1954). Maurice W. Armstrong, *The Great Awakening in Nova Scotia, 1776–1809* (Hartford 1948) really has Alline as its hero and central focus, and is a superb piece of scholarship. Armstrong's view of Alline is far more sympathetic than the one to be found in the opening chapter of S. D. Clark,

Church and Sect in Canada (Toronto 1948). A fascinat-
ing and provocative brief interpretation of Alline's career
is that by George Rawlyk and Gordon Stewart, 'Nova
Scotia's Sense of Mission,' *Social History/Histoire sociale*,
number 2 (November 1968), 5–17. The best available
assessment of Alline as a literary figure – tantalizingly
brief – is by Fred Cogswell in Carl F. Klinck *et al.*, eds.,
*Literary History of Canada: Canadian Literature in
English* (Toronto 1965), 74–77.

The literature on the New England background both
of settlement in Nova Scotia and of religion is enormous.
Among the most useful works are Edmund S. Morgan,
Visible Saints: The History of a Puritan Idea (New York
1963); Richard S. Bushman, *From Puritan and Yankee:
Character and the Social Order In Connecticut, 1690–
1765,* and M. W. Armstrong, 'Backgrounds of Religious
Liberty in Nova Scotia,' *Nova Scotia Historical Society
Collections,* xxvii (1947), 17–32. For the Great Awaken-
ing in New England, see Edmund S. Gaustad, *The Great
Awakening in New England* (New York 1957); C. C.
Goen, *Revivalism and Separatism in New England* (New
Haven 1962); Alan Heimert, *Religion and the American
Mind: From the Great Awakening to the Revolution*
(Cambridge, Mass., 1966), and William G. McLoughlin,
Isaac Backus and the American Pietistic Tradition
(Boston 1966). An extremely provocative essay on causes
of the Awakening is provided by Philip J. Greven, Jr.,
'Family Mobility, and Revivalism in Early America:
Some Perspectives and Hypotheses,' paper read at the
Southern Historical Association meetings in New Orleans,
1968. For a review of recent literature, see J. M. Bumsted,
'What Must I do to be Saved? A Consideration of Recent
Writings on the Great Awakening in Colonial America,'

Bulletin of the Canadian Association of American Studies, spring/summer, 1968. Autobiographical writings such as Alline's account of his conversion are discussed by Daniel B. Shea, Jr., *Spiritual Autobiography in Early America* (Princeton, NJ, 1968); Shea does not consider Alline, however.

The classic monograph on pre-Loyalist Nova Scotia is John B. Brebner's *The Neutral Yankees of Nova Scotia: A Marginal Colony during the Revolutionary Years* (New York 1937). Other published works of importance include I. F. Mackinnon, *Settlements and Churches in Nova Scotia 1749–1776* (Montreal 1930) and W. S. MacNutt, *The Atlantic Provinces: The Emergence of Colonial Society, 1712–1857* (Toronto 1965), especially 53–75. Two of the most important studies remain unpublished: J. S. Martell, 'Pre-Loyalist Settlements around Minas Basin' (unpublished MA thesis, Dalhousie University, 1933), and K. R. Williams, 'Social Conditions in Nova Scotia 1749–1783' (unpublished MA thesis, McGill University, 1936).

The best contemporary sources are John Robinson and Thomas Rispin, *Journey through Nova Scotia containing a particular Account of the Country and its Inhabitants* (York 1774; reprinted in *Report of the Board of Trustees of the Public Archives of Nova Scotia* 1944, 26–57); the first two volumes of the *Diary of Simeon Perkins* (Toronto 1948, 1958); Carl Bridenbaugh, ed., 'Patrick M' Robert's *Tour through Part of the North Provinces of America,*' *Pennsylvania Magazine of History and Biography,* LIX (1935), 153–158; Edward Winslow?, 'Sketch of the Province of Nova Scotia, and chiefly of such parts as are settled, 1783,' *New Brunswick Historical Society Collection,* II, 142–162; and *A Narativ of the*

*Voyage of Tho's Curtis to the Island of St. John's ... in
the year 1775 ...,* in D. C. Harvey, ed., *Journeys to the
Island of St. John* (Toronto 1958), 9–69.

In studying the early period of settlement in the Mari-
times, the various local histories of communities, counties,
and regions are indispensable. Most of these are listed in
W. F. E. Morley, *Canadian Local Histories to 1950: A
Bibliography*; I, *The Atlantic Provinces* (Toronto 1967).
Two local histories which were of particular value for
the study of Alline are John V. Duncanson, *Falmouth:
A New England Township in Nova Scotia* (Windsor,
Ont., 1965) and A. W. H. Eaton, *History of Kings
County, Nova Scotia: Heart of the Acadian Land* (Salem
1910).

The only full-length study of Nova Scotia during the
war of the American Revolution is W. B. Kerr, *The
Maritime Provinces of British North America and the
American Revolution* (Sackville, NB, 1941); the issues
of the critical years are considered in readings edited by
George A. Rawlyk, *Revolution Rejected, 1775–1776*
(Scarborough 1968), 9–54.

Works on the early history of the various religious
denominations in British North America are plentiful.
For the Methodists, see T. W. Smith, *History of
Methodism in Eastern British America* (Halifax 1877)
and Goldwin S. French, *Parsons and Politics: The Role
of the Wesleyan Methodists in Upper Canada and the
Maritimes from 1780 to 1855* (Toronto 1962). For the
Baptists, consult I. E. Bill, *Fifty Years with the Baptist
Ministers and Churches of the Maritime Provinces*
(Halifax 1902), and G. E. Levy, *The Baptists of the
Maritime Provinces, 1753–1946* (Saint John 1946). The

Presbyterian story is told in William Gregg, *History of the Presbyterian Church in Canada* (Toronto 1885).

Most of Alline's important contemporaries have been examined by scholars. The classic study of William Law is J. H. Overton, *William Law, Nonjuror and Mystic ... A Sketch of his Life, Character, and Opinions* (London 1881). The relationship between Law and John Wesley is analysed in Eric W. Baker, *A Herald of the Evangelical Revival: A Critical Inquiry into the Relation of William Law to John Wesley and the Beginnings of Methodism* (London 1948). For Jacob Boehme, consult Hans L. Martensen and Stephen Hobhouse, *Jacob Boehme (1575–1624): Studies in his Life and Teaching* (London 1949). For Alline's Nova Scotia contemporaries, see Matthew Richey, *A Memoir of the Late Rev. William Black, Wesleyan Minister* (Halifax 1839); M. W. Armstrong, ' "Elder Moulton" and the Nova Scotia Baptists,' *Dalhousie Review*, XXIV (1944), 320–323; and C. B. Fergusson, ed., *The Life of Jonathan Scott* (Halifax 1960). An obviously important source for understanding Alline's relationship to his contemporaries is Scott's *A Brief View of the Religious Tenets and Sentiments ... of Mr. Henry Alline* (Halifax 1784). This work is discussed at length in M. W. Armstrong, 'Jonathan Scott's "Brief View," ' *Harvard Theological Review*, XL (1947), 121–136. For the American Freewill Baptists, perhaps Alline's closest doctrinal disciples, see John Buzzell, *The Life of the Elder Benjamin Randall* (Limerick, Maine, 1827), and Norman Baxter, *History of the Freewill Baptists: A Study in New England Separatism* (Rochester 1957).

INDEX

This book
was designed by
ANTJE LINGNER
under the direction of
ALLAN FLEMING
and was printed by
University of
Toronto
Press